D1370085

Amphetamines and Other Stimulants

JUNIOR DRUG AWARENESS

JUNIOR DRUG AWARENESS

Amphetamines and Other Stimulants

Lianne Warburton and Diana Callfas

CHELSEA HOUSE
PUBLISHERS
An imprint of Infobase Publishing

Junior Drug Awareness: Amphetamines and Other Stimulants

Copyright © 2008 by Infobase Publishing

All rights reserved. No part of this book may be reproduced or utilized in any form or by any means, electronic or mechanical, including photocopying, recording, or by any information storage or retrieval systems, without permission in writing from the publisher. For information contact:

Chelsea House
An imprint of Infobase Publishing
132 West 31st Street
New York NY 10001

Library of Congress Cataloging-in-Publication Data

Warburton, Lianne.
  Amphetamines and other stimulants / Lianne Warburton and Diana Callfas.
     p. cm. — (Junior Drug Awareness)
  Includes bibliographical references and index.
  ISBN-13: 978-0-7910-9712-0 (hardcover)
  ISBN-10: 0-7910-9712-9 (hardcover)
  1. Amphetamine abuse—Juvenile literature. 2. Stimulants—Juvenile literature. I. Callfas, Diana. II. Title. III. Series.

  RC568.A45W37 2008
  362.29'9—dc22   2007018860

Chelsea House books are available at special discounts when purchased in bulk quantities for businesses, associations, institutions, or sales promotions. Please call our Special Sales Department in New York at (212) 967-8800 or (800) 322-8755.

You can find Chelsea House on the World Wide Web
at http://www.chelseahouse.com

All links and web addresses were checked and verified to be correct at the time of publication. Because of the dynamic nature of the web, some addresses and links may have changed since publication and may no longer be valid.

Series design by Erik Lindstrom
Cover design by Jooyoung An

Printed in the United States of America

Bang FOF 10 9 8 7 6 5 4 3 2 1

This book is printed on acid-free paper.

CONTENTS

Battling a Pandemic: A History of Drugs in the United States

When Johnny came marching home again after the Civil War, he probably wasn't marching in a very straight line. This is because Johnny, like 400,000 of his fellow drug-addled soldiers, was addicted to morphine. With the advent of morphine and the invention of the hypodermic needle, drug addiction became a prominent problem during the nineteenth century. It was the first time such widespread drug dependence was documented in history.

Things didn't get much better in the later decades of the nineteenth century. Cocaine and opiates were used as over-the-counter "medicines." Of course, the most famous was Coca-Cola, which actually did contain cocaine in its early days.

After the turn of the twentieth century, drug abuse was spiraling out of control, and the United States government stepped in with the first regulatory controls. In 1906, the Pure Food and Drug Act became a law. It required the labeling of product ingredients. Next came the Harrison Narcotics Tax Act of 1914, which outlawed illegal importation or distribution of cocaine and opiates. During this time, neither the medical community nor the general population was aware of the principles of addiction.

After the passage of the Harrison Act, drug addiction was not a major issue in the United States until the 1960s, when drug abuse became a much bigger social problem. During this time, the federal government's drug enforcement agencies were found to be ineffective. Organizations often worked against one another, causing counterproductive effects. By 1973, things had gotten so bad that President Richard Nixon, by executive order, created the Drug Enforcement Administration (DEA), which became the lead agency in all federal narcotics investigations. It continues in that role to this day. The effectiveness of enforcement and the so-called "Drug War" are open to debate. Cocaine use has been reduced by 75% since its peak in 1985. However, its replacement might be methamphetamine (speed, crank, crystal), which is arguably more dangerous and is now plaguing the country. Also, illicit drugs tend to be cyclical, with various drugs, such as LSD, appearing, disappearing, and then reappearing again. It is probably closest to the truth to say that a war on drugs can never be won, just managed.

Fighting drugs involves a three-pronged battle. Enforcement is one prong. Education and prevention is the second. Treatment is the third.

Although pandemics of drug abuse have been with us for more than 150 years, education and prevention were not seriously considered until the 1970s. In 1982, former First Lady Betty Ford made drug treatment socially acceptable with the opening of the Betty Ford Center. This followed her own battle with addiction. Other treatment centers—including Hazelton, Fair Oaks, and Smithers (now called the Addiction Institute of New York)—added to the growing number of clinics, and soon detox facilities were in almost every city. The cost of a single day in one of these facilities is often more than $1,000, and the effectiveness of treatment centers is often debated. To this day, there is little regulation over who can practice counseling.

It soon became apparent that the most effective way to deal with the drug problem was prevention by education. By some estimates, the overall cost of drug abuse to society exceeds $250 billion per year; preventive education is certainly the most cost-effective way to deal with the problem. Drug education can save people from misery, pain, and ultimately even jail time or death. In the early 1980s, First Lady Nancy Reagan started the "Just Say No" program. Although many scoffed at the program, its promotion of total abstinence from drugs has been effective with many adolescents. In the late 1980s, drug education was not science based, and people essentially were throwing mud at the wall to see what would stick. Motivations of all types spawned hundreds, if not thousands, of drug-education programs. Promoters of some programs used whatever political clout they could muster to get on various government agencies' lists of most effective programs. The bottom line, however, is that prevention is very difficult to quantify. How do you prove that drug use would have occurred if it were not prevented from happening?

In 1983, the Los Angeles Unified School District, in conjunction with the Los Angeles Police Department, started what was considered at that time to be the gold standard of school-based drug education programs. The program was called Drug Abuse Resistance Education, otherwise known as D.A.R.E. The program called for specially trained police officers to deliver drug-education programs in schools. This was an era in which community-oriented policing was all the rage. The logic was that kids would give street credibility to a police officer who spoke to them about drugs. The popularity of the program was unprecedented. It spread all across the country and around the world. Ultimately, 80% of American school districts would utilize the program. Parents, police officers, and kids all loved it. Unexpectedly, a special bond was formed between the kids who took the program and the police officers who ran it. Even in adulthood, many kids remember the name of their D.A.R.E. officer.

By 1991, national drug use had been halved. In any other medical-oriented field, this figure would be astonishing. The number of people in the United States using drugs went from about 25 million in the early 1980s to 11 million in 1991. All three prongs of the battle against drugs vied for government dollars, with each prong claiming credit for the reduction in drug use. There is no doubt that each contributed to the decline in drug use, but most people agreed that preventing drug abuse before it started had proved to be the most effective strategy. The National Institute on Drug Abuse (NIDA), which was established in 1974, defines its mandate in this way: "NIDA's mission is to lead the Nation in bringing the power of science to bear on drug abuse and addiction." NIDA leaders were the experts in prevention and treatment, and they had enormous resources. In

1986, the nonprofit Partnership for a Drug-Free America was founded. The organization defined its mission as, "Putting to use all major media outlets, including TV, radio, print advertisements and the Internet, along with the pro bono work of the country's best advertising agencies." The Partnership for a Drug-Free America is responsible for the popular campaign that compared "your brain on drugs" to fried eggs.

The American drug problem was front-page news for years up until 1990–1991. Then the Gulf War took over the news, and drugs never again regained the headlines. Most likely, this lack of media coverage has led to some peaks and valleys in the number of people using drugs, but there has not been a return to anything near the high percentage of use recorded in 1985. According to the University of Michigan's 2006 Monitoring the Future study, which measured adolescent drug use, there were 840,000 fewer American kids using drugs in 2006 than in 2001. This represents a 23% reduction in drug use. With the exception of prescription drugs, drug use continues to decline.

In 2000, the Robert Wood Johnson Foundation recognized that the D.A.R.E. Program, with its tens of thousands of trained police officers, had the top state-of-the-art delivery system of drug education in the world. The foundation dedicated $15 million to develop a cutting-edge prevention curriculum to be delivered by D.A.R.E. The new D.A.R.E. program incorporates the latest in prevention and education, including high-tech, interactive, and decision-model-based approaches. D.A.R.E. officers are trained as "coaches" who support kids as they practice research-based refusal strategies in high-stakes peer-pressure environments. Through stunning magnetic resonance imaging (MRI) images, students get to see tangible proof of how various substances diminish brain activity.

Will this program be the solution to the drug problem in the United States? By itself, probably not. It is simply an integral part of a larger equation that everyone involved hopes will prevent kids from ever starting to use drugs. The equation also requires guidance in the home, without which no program can be effective.

Ronald J. Brogan
Regional Director
D.A.R.E America

The Truth About Stimulants

In early 2004, two people kidnapped and tortured a man. They thought the man had stolen $125 worth of **methamphetamine**—an addictive and dangerous **stimulant** drug—from them. The man was attacked with a hammer, pliers, and a sword.

That same year, a 19-year-old man was sentenced to 30 years in jail for homicide after he ran over three siblings with his car. He was driving under the influence of a stimulant. As a result of the crash, a six-year-old boy was paralyzed and his brother and sister were killed.

In 2005, Charles James Hickman was arrested after the body of a 10-year-old girl was found in a creek just outside her hometown. The girl was reported missing when she did not return home after running an errand.

Hickman admitted to kidnapping the child. He told police that he wanted to scare her so she would keep quiet about seeing some methamphetamine in an apartment near her home.

WHAT IS A STIMULANT?

There are many kinds of stimulants. **Caffeine, nicotine, cocaine, Ecstasy,** methamphetamine (**crystal meth**) and **Ritalin** are all stimulants, but some are milder and less toxic (less poisonous) than others. They may affect different areas of the body in different ways.

Caffeine is found in chocolate bars, soda, and energy drinks such as Red Bull. These items are commonly available and are consumed by millions of people each day. Caffeine can make people's hearts beat faster and make them feel more alert and energetic. It is not usually considered dangerous unless it is consumed in very large amounts.

Nicotine is another commonly used stimulant. It is found in cigarettes and chewing tobacco. Nicotine increases blood pressure and makes the heart beat faster. People who use nicotine say it makes them feel relaxed. Anyone using nicotine can develop an **addiction** to it. This means that a person's body needs nicotine to function normally.

Smoking is linked with heart attacks and strokes. It is a common cause of lung disease and cancer. Smoking also can cause stained teeth and wrinkled skin. Using chewing tobacco increases the risks of cancers of the mouth, throat, voice box, and esophagus. Chewing tobacco also is linked with gum damage and tooth loss.

Despite these effects, many people, including young people, buy and use cigarettes and chewing tobacco every day. Many of these people are addicted. Some

Nicotine is a highly addictive stimulant that is found in all tobacco products, such as cigarettes, chewing tobacco, and cigars. Immediate effects of nicotine include increased heart rate and blood pressure. Long-term use of tobacco products could cause lung, throat, or other cancers. Above, a healthy lung (left) is pictured next to a smoker's lung (right).

studies show that nicotine may be more addictive than heroin or cocaine. People who try to stop using it often become angry, irritable, or depressed. Even though they know they should quit, they often decide to continue smoking or using chewing tobacco to stop these negative feelings. Also, because nicotine can reduce appetite, people trying to stop using nicotine may feel hungry all the time. Tobacco products are so dangerous that laws prevent them from being sold to people younger than a certain age (usually 18 or 19).

Other stimulants—including **amphetamines**, methamphetamine (crystal meth), Ritalin (**methylphe-**

nidate), cocaine, and Ecstasy (methylenedioxymethamphetamine, or **MDMA**)—are powerful and dangerous. These drugs are highly addictive and often are abused. Many people buy, sell, and use these drugs illegally. However, these medications are not always abused: Sometimes doctors prescribe them to treat illnesses.

Ritalin and some of the amphetamines (including **dextroamphetamine** and mixed amphetamine salts) are used to treat **attention-deficit/hyperactivity disorder (ADHD)**. In addition to Ritalin, other examples of these types of medications are **Adderall**, **Dexedrine**, and **Concerta**. When used properly, these drugs can help people with ADHD to focus their attention. These drugs also can decrease hyperactivity (an excess of energy or activity) or reckless and "bad" behavior. Some of these prescription stimulants are also used to help people with **narcolepsy**. Narcolepsy is a condition that causes people to fall asleep quickly at unusual times, such as while driving. Amphetamines also may be used to treat obesity (the condition of being very overweight), because these drugs decrease hunger and help the body to break down food more quickly. Newer stimulants such as **Meridia (sibutramine)** often are tried first to treat obesity because these newer drugs are safer and less addictive than amphetamines.

Doctors in some countries still prescribe cocaine and methamphetamine. Methamphetamine is sometimes used to treat severe cases of narcolepsy and ADHD. In Europe, cocaine is used as a local anesthetic to numb an area of skin.

Psychiatrists once used Ecstasy (MDMA) to help their patients during therapy sessions. Ecstasy became illegal in the 1980s, however, and is no longer used for traditional medical purposes. Research scientists are allowed

(continues on page 18)

PSEUDOEPHEDRINE AND EPHEDRINE: THE GOOD, THE BAD, AND THE UGLY

THE GOOD

Pseudoephedrine is a stimulant that is widely used to treat the common cold. It is a nasal **decongestant** (a medicine that helps to unplug the nose). When used properly, it works well and is very safe. It can be bought without a prescription.

Ephedrine is another commonly used stimulant that can be purchased legally in small amounts. Like pseudoephedrine, ephedrine is used as a nasal decongestant. It may also help people with asthma by opening up their airways. Some people use products that contain ephedrine or its herbal equivalent, ephedra, to try to lose weight or stay awake. Ephedrine is more dangerous then pseudoephedrine because of its effects on the heart and blood vessels. Recently, governments in some countries have put laws into place that limit the amounts of ephedrine that can be sold.

THE BAD

Pseudoephedrine and ephedrine are stimulant drugs. They have side effects, including shakiness and **insomnia**. These drugs can be dangerous if they are used by people who are taking other medications or by individuals who have certain diseases or illnesses. For example, pseudoephedrine and ephedrine can make blood pressure medications work less effectively. They may also cause the heart to speed up too much. This can be especially dangerous for people who already have heart problems.

People who do not have any health problems also can be badly affected by these stimulants. This usually happens

Many over-the-counter cold and allergy medicines contain the stimulants pseudoephedrine and ephedrine, which are ingredients commonly used to make methamphetamine. In order to combat the growing meth problem, a store in Roseville, Michigan, began putting product identification cards in place of the medicine so young customers could not purchase the drugs without showing identification. By state law, only customers 17 years of age or older may buy over-the-counter medicines such as Sudafed and Claritin-D, and adult customers may only purchase two packages per visit.

when people take more of these products then they should. It may also happen when pseudoephedrine and ephedrine are mixed with other drugs, including the stimulants nicotine and caffeine. Finally, sometimes people have bad side

(continues on page 18)

(continued from page 17)

effects from these drugs even when they use them exactly as directed.

THE UGLY

In 2001, a player on the Minnesota Vikings football team had a heart attack and died during training camp. It is believed that his ephedra use led to his death. In 2003, Steve Bechler, a 23-year-old pitcher for the Baltimore Orioles, died of heatstroke. His death also was linked with ephedrine. Many teenagers and young adults also have died because of these drugs. Sean Riggins was a 16-year-old football player and wrestler from Illinois. He died after his heart stopped. He was taking Yellow Jackets, a supplement that contains ephedra. A 19-year-old college student started taking ephedrine to stay awake. One day later, he had a fatal heart attack while he was pumping gas. He had taken only four capsules of the drug.

Pseudoephedrine and ephedrine are also now being used as ingredients to make crystal meth, the highly addictive and dangerous street drug.

(continued from page 15)

to give the drug to small groups of people who have certain illnesses to study how the drug works and how it affects people.

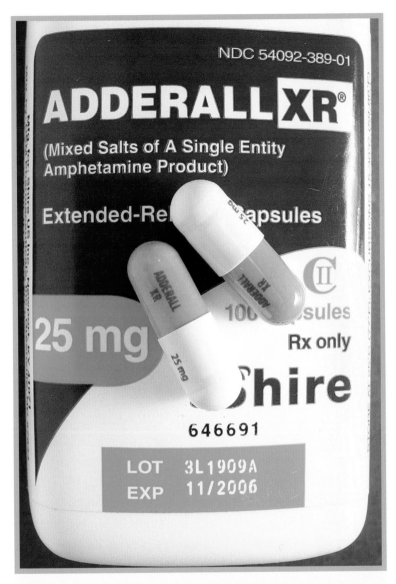

Adderall is a common stimulant amphetamine used to treat attention-deficit/hyperactivity disorder (ADHD). Adderall helps focus a person's attention, which is why it is a popular drug on college campuses. Students who may or may not suffer from ADHD use the drug recreationally so they can stay up all night and cram before exams.

THE LIFE OF AN ILLEGAL DRUG

Although most stimulants started out as medicines, many now are being used and sold illegally. Most people get illegal drugs from dealers, but some people get these drugs by going to a doctor and getting a prescription. Other people make their drugs. Some people steal drugs, and some **smuggle** them in from other countries.

Cocaine is smuggled into the United States from Colombia, South America, and other tropical countries. Cocaine comes from the leaves of the coca plant, which grows only in warm climates. To avoid being caught with drugs, some smugglers swallow many small packages of cocaine and bring them across the border in their stomachs. These people are called mules because they carry drugs to one place from another like mules in an old-fashioned mule train.

Once over the border, the mules are given medicines called laxatives. Laxatives, which also can be stimulants, normally are used to treat constipation. When people take laxatives, their stomachs start to cramp, and they have to go to the bathroom. After the mules' bodies eliminate the smuggled drugs, the mules or the drug dealers who are their bosses repackage and sell the drugs. Bringing drugs into the country this way is very dangerous. Mules can die if the drug packages break while they are in their bodies. The smugglers also risk being caught by border guards and police.

This is not the only way that cocaine is smuggled. Some smugglers hide drugs in secret compartments in cars, airplanes, or boats. Some invent new and different ways to bring in drugs. Although border guards and the police catch a number of smugglers each year, other smugglers still manage to bring cocaine into the United States across borders and through airports and seaports.

In 2005, Brazilian law officers discovered a truck filled with two tons of cocaine hidden inside frozen meat. Although there are strict laws against it, illegal drug smuggling is a challenging crime to combat. Drug smugglers use many different ways to transport drugs, which makes it extremely difficult to catch them and find illegal drugs.

Ritalin and most amphetamines usually are not smuggled. Instead, people get these drugs through **prescription forgeries** (fake prescriptions), buy them legally, or buy them from someone who has stolen them from a pharmacy. People also can get methamphetamine in these ways, but most methamphetamine found today is in the form of crystal meth.

Crystal meth and Ecstasy are produced in **clandestine** (illegal and hidden) **labs** by "**street chemists**" and dealers. These drugs may be made locally, or they may be made in other countries (such as Mexico) and then smuggled over the border.

Buyers can never really know what is in street drugs or how they will affect someone who takes them. Medicines prescribed by a doctor have been tested for many years to make sure that they are safe. Street drugs are never tested at all. When street drugs are made, dangerous **contaminants** can be left behind in the final product. For example, lead (a dangerous heavy metal) can be left behind in methamphetamine when it is made. Lead poisoning damages the heart, kidneys, and brain, and can lead to death.

A street chemist also may alter the chemical structures of a drug to change the way it works and how long it stays in the body. This can increase a drug's dangerous effects. Finally, many of the people who are making drugs are doing so while they are "**high**" themselves. They also may take unsafe shortcuts to increase their profits.

THE EFFECTS OF STIMULANTS

All stimulants cause certain changes in the body. Even stimulants prescribed by a doctor, or the caffeine that you drink, can cause some of these changes. When a person uses a stimulant, he or she can experience both **central** and **peripheral effects.**

Central effects involve the brain and nervous system. These effects occur because of changes in the levels of **chemical messengers** in the brain. Central effects may alter the way a person feels or acts and also may change the way that person sees and reacts to the things around him or her. Stimulants can make a user feel alert and full of energy. They can increase a person's metabolism—which can cause weight loss—and can make a person feel happy and motivated and thus able to get more work done.

Peripheral effects involve the heart, muscles, kidneys, and other organs besides the brain. Peripheral effects include increases in blood pressure and heart rate. At first, these changes may make a person feel hyperactive. Over time, however, they can lead to shakiness, headache, agitation, and heavy sweating.

CHEMICAL MESSENGERS AND THE BRAIN

Stimulants have such powerful effects because they work directly inside the brain. The brain acts as a control center for the entire body. This control center is made up of billions of cells called **neurons** that send messages to all parts of the body. To understand how stimulants affect the brain, it is important to learn what a neuron looks like and how it works.

The most important part of a neuron is the **cell body**, the part that contains the **nucleus**. Every cell has a nucleus, which is responsible for directing the traffic of that cell. Individual cells learn what to do based on messages sent from neighboring cells. Neighboring neurons talk to each other using **dendrites** and **axons**. Dendrites are short fibers on one side of a neuron. The dendrites receive messages sent by nearby cells. These messages then are sent to the cell body. In the cell body,

(continues on page 27)

THE DURATION OF EFFECTS OF ADDICTIVE DRUGS

Drugs stay in the body for different amounts of time. The length of time that a user can feel the effects of a drug depends on several things:

- what type of drug it is
- how much the person took
- the person's level of **tolerance** (how used to the drug the person's body has become)
- what else is present in the drug
- other drugs the person has taken at the same time

DRUG	HOW LONG DO THE EFFECTS LAST?	FOR HOW LONG CAN THE DRUG BE DETECTED IN THE BODY?
STIMULANTS		
Methamphetamine	The effects of meth-amphetamine last for about 6 to 12 hours, which is a lot longer than most other drugs.	Methamphetamine usually can be detected in the urine for about 2 to 4 days after drug use is stopped.
Amphetamines	The effects of amphetamines may last for up to 12 hours if they are taken in average doses.	Like methamphet-amine, the other amphetamines can be detected in the urine for up to 4 days after the drug use is stopped.

Ritalin	Ritalin's effects last for about 3 to 4 hours.	Ritalin usually is removed from the body in about 3 days.
Cocaine	The effects of cocaine are immediate but short-lived. Effects last anywhere from 5 minutes to 3 hours.	Cocaine usually can be detected in the urine for about 3 days after drug use is stopped.
Ecstasy	The effects of Ecstasy start in about 1 hour and usually last for about 6 hours. Some people have reported feeling the effects for many days after drug use was stopped.	Ecstasy can be detected in the urine for up to 4 days after drug use is stopped.
Caffeine	The effects of caffeine begin in about 5 minutes, peak (reach maximum effect) in about 30 minutes, and last for about 3 to 4 hours.	Caffeine is not routinely tested for (except in athletes). Most caffeine is eliminated from the body within 15 to 35 hours.
Nicotine	When smoked, nicotine may reach the brain and cause effects in 8 seconds. People feel the effects of nicotine for only a few minutes.	Nicotine can be detected in the urine for up to 3 days after use.

(continues on page 26)

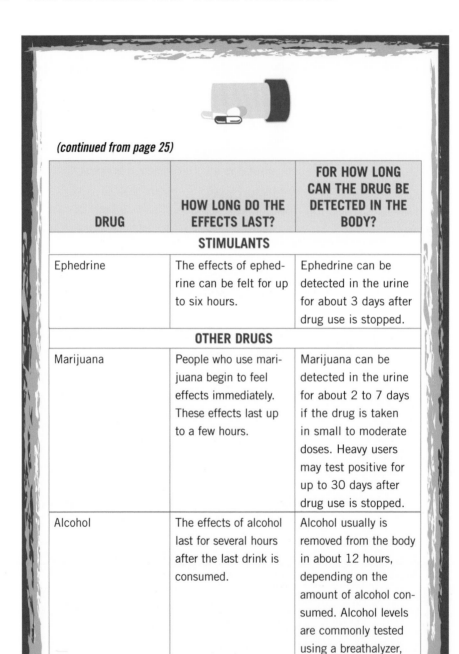

(continued from page 25)

DRUG	HOW LONG DO THE EFFECTS LAST?	FOR HOW LONG CAN THE DRUG BE DETECTED IN THE BODY?
STIMULANTS		
Ephedrine	The effects of ephedrine can be felt for up to six hours.	Ephedrine can be detected in the urine for about 3 days after drug use is stopped.
OTHER DRUGS		
Marijuana	People who use marijuana begin to feel effects immediately. These effects last up to a few hours.	Marijuana can be detected in the urine for about 2 to 7 days if the drug is taken in small to moderate doses. Heavy users may test positive for up to 30 days after drug use is stopped.
Alcohol	The effects of alcohol last for several hours after the last drink is consumed.	Alcohol usually is removed from the body in about 12 hours, depending on the amount of alcohol consumed. Alcohol levels are commonly tested using a breathalyzer, not a urine test.
Heroin	The effects of heroin can be felt for between 2 and 6 hours.	Heroin can be detected in the urine for 1 to 2 days after drug use is stopped.

(continued from page 23)

the nucleus decodes the message and sends a signal down the axon. The axon is a single, long nerve fiber.

The axon of one neuron does not actually touch the dendrites of a neighboring neuron. Because of this, the body needs a way for the message to "jump" from one neuron to the next across a tiny gap. This is where **neurotransmitters** come in. Neurotransmitters are chemical messengers. When a signal comes down an axon, the axon releases neurotransmitters into the tiny gap between it and the dendrites of other neurons. This tiny gap is called a **synapse**. The neurotransmitters travel across the synapse and bind to certain spots on the dendrites of nearby cells. These special binding spots are called **receptors**. Once the neurotransmitters bind to the receptors, the message has been sent. Then, the neurotransmitters may be **metabolized** (broken down) in the synapse. The neurotransmitters also may be taken up by the axon that released them and eventually used again. This recycling process is referred to as **neurotransmitter reuptake**.

Many types of neurotransmitters work in the brain, but only a few are affected by stimulant drugs. The most important of these affected neurotransmitters is **dopamine**. Dopamine is called the pleasure neurotransmitter. It is released when a person is involved in activities that he or she thinks are rewarding. A player who has just scored the winning run in a baseball game probably feels happy. That's because neurons in the player's brain have released dopamine. The dopamine binds to receptors on nearby dendrites, and the "happy signal" keeps moving through the player's brain. After the excitement ends, the dopamine is either broken down, or is taken up again by the axons that released it. Stimulant drugs also cause high levels of dopamine to be released. Thus, users feel happier when they take these drugs.

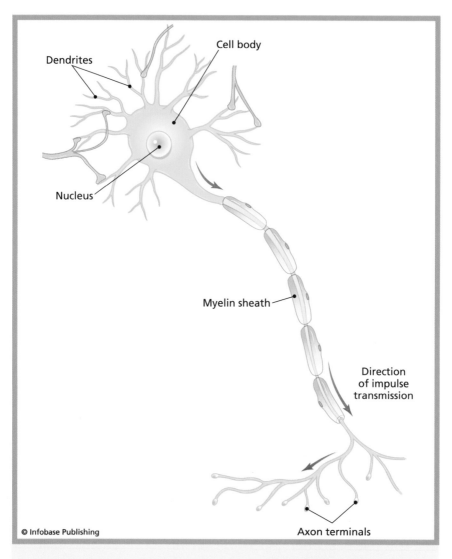

Dendrites

Cell body

Nucleus

Myelin sheath

Direction of impulse transmission

© Infobase Publishing

Axon terminals

A neuron consists of a cell body, axon, and dendrites. The cell body contains a nucleus, which is the control center of the neuron. Axons carry nerve impulses away from the cell body. They are often wrapped in myelin, which helps increase the speed of impulse transmission. Dendrites receive nerve impulses from adjacent neurons.

Another neurotransmitter that is increased by stimulant drugs is **norepinephrine**. This transmitter controls the **fight-or-flight response**, which determines how the body will respond to emergency situations. In times of stress, norepinephrine increases the heart rate, expands the airways, provides fuel for muscles, and makes the pupils in the eyes get bigger. These changes lead a person either to run away from a stressful situation or stay and fight it out.

Stimulants also may affect the release of the neurotransmitter **serotonin** in the brain. Serotonin levels can affect how hungry you are, how aggressive or angry you are, how well you sleep, and your general mood. Higher levels of serotonin make you feel good. They also can lead to changes in vision or make physical contact feel better than it usually does. Large amounts of serotonin are released in the brain when people use Ecstasy.

Amphetamines have a powerful effect on the brain because they are chemically similar to the brain's neurotransmitters. In fact, amphetamines can enter the axons of neurons just as dopamine and norepinephrine can. Once an amphetamine enters an axon, there is not enough room for both the drug and the neurotransmitter, so the neurotransmitter is "kicked out" into the synapse. When this happens, the neurotransmitter can bind to dendrites and start sending messages. Stimulant drugs also stop neurotransmitters from being taken up again into the axon for recycling. This creates an even bigger response in the brain.

Other stimulant drugs also work by affecting the brain's neurotransmitters. Like the amphetamines, Ritalin and cocaine stop neurotransmitter reuptake. However, they do not enter the axons, which is why their effects do not last as long as the amphetamines. Caffeine and nicotine may also affect neurotransmitters such as dopamine, but their main effects are due to other complicated changes in the brain.

2

Stimulants Make History

Although amphetamines have become mainstream only recently, they have been around for more than 100 years. Amphetamine was first produced in Germany in 1887. Methamphetamine was discovered in Japan in 1893. It was not until the 1930s, however, that these drugs were used in medicine. Amphetamine was first marketed as a nasal decongestant inhaler called Benzedrine. The drug's stimulant effects—such as increased energy, alertness, and **euphoria**—soon were recognized, and new forms of the drug emerged. Many of these new drugs were available without a prescription. At that time, amphetamines were used to treat such conditions as obesity, asthma, bed-wetting, narcolepsy, depression, and heroin addiction. Amphetamines were even used to treat such things as constant hiccups.

During World War II, soldiers from many countries took amphetamines and methamphetamine to improve their confidence and endurance. Chocolates containing methamphetamine were given to German pilots and tanker troops, and German dictator Adolf Hitler received daily injections of the drug to treat depression.

Following World War II, amphetamine use became common among returning soldiers. Amphetamines also became popular with other groups, including homemakers, who used the drugs to boost energy and for weight loss. Truckers used amphetamines to help them stay awake on long trips. Even athletes began adding these energy-enhancing drugs to their training programs. With this increase in amphetamine use, people in all areas of society began to witness the addictive properties and dangerous side effects of these drugs.

During the 1960s and 1970s, in response to growing concern about amphetamines' effects on health, lawmakers and government officials began to take some of these drugs off the market. At the same time, governments also tightened the laws affecting the drugs that were left. Soon, illegal production of methamphetamine began to increase to keep up with the demand for the drug. Motorcycle gangs quickly became an important source of illegal methamphetamine in North America. Gangs in California trained their members to make methamphetamine in clandestine labs, and this illegal activity quickly spread eastward.

By the 1980s, the use and production of methamphetamine had spread from California to the Southwest and Midwest. (A similar eastward trend also was observed in

(continues on page 34)

DOPING IN SPORTS

Sports **doping** began in ancient times and it continues today. Doping is a term that is used to describe the use of drugs or banned substances by athletes to enhance their physical performance or to gain a competitive edge. Doping is not allowed in amateur and professional sports. Athletes are routinely tested for drugs both during and outside of competition. If athletes are caught using drugs they can be disqualified or may be banned from their sport forever.

The reasons for doping are different for every athlete but often include some of the following:

- Addiction
- Easy access to the drugs
- To improve the athlete's performance
- Ego or a very strong desire to win
- Peer pressure or pressure from family, coaches, or the media
- To remain competitive with other athletes who are using the drugs

Also, sometimes people take drugs such as stimulants without meaning to or without realizing that they are taking them. This happens because some stimulants are ingredients in sodas, cold medications, herbal products, and energy drinks.

Drugs have been banned in sports because they are illegal outside the world of sports and/or they give users an advantage over their competition. Plus, many drugs have dangerous side effects. These dangers become even greater

In the 2006 Winter Olympic Games, Russian biathlete Olga Pyleva was stripped of her silver medal after she tested positive for carphedon, a strictly prohibited stimulant. Pyleva claimed that the stimulant was in an over-the-counter medicine she took to treat an injured ankle. Although she has maintained her innocence, she was stripped of her medal, expelled from the games, and banned from two years of competition.

if the drugs are not used correctly, which may happen when they are used to improve performance.

Banned substances may vary from sport to sport but often include:

- Stimulants: Amphetamines, methamphetamine, pseudoephedrine, ephedrine, and caffeine (when taken amounts that are equal to five cups of coffee or more)
- Steroids
- Hormones

(continues on page 34)

(continued from page 33)

- Beta-blockers (drugs that are prescribed to treat blood pressure and some heart conditions)
- Alcohol
- Diuretics (drugs that are prescribed to treat blood pressure and remove extra fluid from the body)
- Narcotics (drugs that are used to treat severe pain)
- Street drugs (includes marijuana, cocaine, heroin, and Ecstasy)

Stimulant abuse is common in intense sports that require short bursts of energy, such as cycling, football, hockey and baseball. Athletes who are involved in long-distance events such as skiing also may turn to stimulants. Stimulants have been shown to improve performance, strength and endurance. They decrease drowsiness and improve reaction time. Amphetamine and amphetamine-like stimulants also may increase an athlete's confidence and desire to win. However, stimulants can be very dangerous. They can cause aggression, high blood pressure, shakiness, seizures, strokes, changes in the way the heart beats, and death. People who are involved in sports are at a greater risk because they are already pushing their bodies beyond "normal" physical limits and often take more of the drug then they should.

(continued from page 31)
Canada.) During this period, large amounts of the drug also were entering the United States from Mexico. The island state of Hawaii received most of its methamphetamine supply from the Philippines and other countries in Asia.

RITALIN: A PRESCRIPTION FOR DISASTER

Methylphenidate, more commonly known as Ritalin, was first discovered in Europe in the 1940s. It was **patented** in the United States in 1954, and was approved by the **Food and Drug Administration (FDA)** one year later. At first, Ritalin was supposed to be a substitute for more powerful and addictive stimulants, such as the amphetamines. It was used to treat conditions that included depression, narcolepsy, and fatigue.

In the 1960s, the FDA approved methylphenidate to treat memory loss in the elderly and behavior problems in children. At first, doctors prescribed methylphenidate only for children who had problems sitting still and also displayed other troublesome behaviors. It was not until the 1980s that doctors devised a name for these behavior problems in children and coined the term **attention deficit disorder (ADD)**. This newly defined disorder included symptoms such as difficulty concentrating and problems with listening. In 1987, the definition of ADD was changed to include symptoms of high energy and reckless actions, and the condition was renamed attention-deficit/hyperactivity disorder (ADHD).

Once these guidelines became well known, doctors began diagnosing more children with ADHD and prescribing more methylphenidate. Ritalin use increased dramatically, partly because it was advertised as safer than amphetamines. Drug companies had to make more methylphenidate to keep up with the demand. And as more methylphenidate became available, illegal use of the drug increased.

Although it is believed that abuse of methylphenidate began much earlier, it was not until the 1960s that drug regulators in several countries realized that the drug could be abused and that people could become addicted

(continues on page 38)

COKE AND THE LOVE DRUG

COKE

The drug cocaine comes from the leaves of the coca plant. People in South America have chewed coca leaves for thousands of years. Among other effects, chewing coca leaves helped people living in Andes Mountain regions to breathe at high altitudes, where less oxygen was available. It was not until the 1800s that the coca plant made its way to other parts of the world. In 1850, the first coca tinctures (medical mixtures) were used during throat surgeries to relieve pain. A few years later, the pharmaceutical drug maker Merck & Company began to produce cocaine. In the 1870s, doctors began using cocaine to treat morphine addiction. During that same period, wines that contained cocaine were made and sold legally. Cocaine also was used as a local anesthetic. Many influential people, including the world-famous psychoanalyst Sigmund Freud, praised the drug and encouraged its use.

As demand for cocaine increased, companies invented new ways to **purify** the drug. Cocaine was even included in a soft drink: Coca-Cola. Introduced in 1886, Coca-Cola (Coke) no longer contains cocaine. The ingredient was removed from the soft drink in the early 1900s after reports began to appear of drug abuse, health problems, and even deaths related to cocaine.

By 1914, the dangers of cocaine had become obvious, and it was banned in the United States. In the 1970s, cocaine reappeared in a new form called "freebase cocaine," "crack cocaine," or, simply, "crack." Cocaine also became common at bars, clubs and discos. In the

A 19th century advertisement promotes the stimulating effect of Coca-Cola. Cocaine was used in the newly developed soft drink before the dangers of the stimulant were well known. The substance was removed from the soft drink after cocaine's harmful effects were better studied.

1980s, the drug became cheaper to buy, and cocaine use exploded. Rumors of many Hollywood stars using the drug and scenes in a number of popular movies, such as *Scarface*, made cocaine use seem cool and glamorous. Cocaine abuse remains a serious problem.

THE LOVE DRUG

Unlike cocaine, Ecstasy is a relatively new drug. There is some debate about why it was first produced. Some say it was designed to be an appetite suppressant. Others believe that it was not intended to be a drug at all. They suggest

(continues on page 38)

(continued from page 37)

that it was made as an ingredient for a drug that would control blood loss. After Ecstasy was patented, in 1914, it "disappeared" for nearly 40 years.

In the 1950s, the United States Army tested Ecstasy on animals. The army kept the results of these tests classified for 20 years. In the 1960s and 1970s, a small group of psychotherapists began using Ecstasy during therapy sessions to relax patients and increase communication. It was during these two decades that "the love drug" also began appearing on the streets. In 1985, Ecstasy became illegal in the United States. In the 1990s, despite the drug's illegal status, Ecstasy became widely available. The drug's use and abuse began in trendy bars and gay dance clubs and quickly spread to the rave scene. Soon Ecstasy was everywhere, including universities and high schools. Today, it is one of the most widely abused drugs.

(continued from page 35)

to it. In 1968, Sweden banned methylphenidate because of widespread street use of the drug.

In the United States today, methylphenidate is prescribed in large quantities and also continues to be sold on the street. In an attempt to reduce illegal use, legal drug makers have produced new forms of methylphenidate, such as Concerta. The methylphenidate in Concerta is enclosed in a special membrane (skin or outer layer) that makes it more difficult to abuse.

3

The Devil's Candy: Crystal Meth and Other Amphetamines

Amphetamines are powerful and highly addictive stimulant drugs. They exist in both legal and illegal forms. When used correctly, amphetamines are helpful in treating numerous medical conditions, including ADHD. However, when these drugs are abused or illegal forms are used, they become dangerous.

Amphetamine is the **parent drug** of related drugs, including dextroamphetamine (Dexedrine, Dextrostat), methamphetamine (Desoxyn), and methylenedioxymethamphetamine (MDMA, or Ecstasy). Adderall is a mixture of amphetamine salts. Crystal meth is an illegal type of methamphetamine.

When prescribed by a doctor, dextroamphetamine, methamphetamine, and mixed amphetamines are available as tablets or capsules. They come in many sizes, shapes, colors, and strengths. Illegal forms of amphetamines vary widely in purity and in how they are made. They have different smells, tastes, appearances, and textures. Crystal meth is a good example. In its purest form, crystal meth looks like clear, shiny shards of glass. However, depending on how it is produced, crystal meth may look like yellow, brown, or pink crystals or granules. It may even appear as a peanut butter–like substance or as "Christmas tree meth," which is bright green in color. (The green comes from Drano crystals that are used in making the drug.) Methamphetamine can also be found in powder, liquid, tablet, or capsule forms. It has a bitter taste and may smell fishy or like cat urine.

HOW AMPHETAMINES ARE USED

Amphetamines can be used in many different ways, and the effects change depending on how they are taken. Most amphetamines can be taken **orally** as tablets, capsules, or liquids. They may also be added to beverages. An unusual way to take amphetamines is called "parachuting." This involves wrapping the drug in a piece of toilet or tissue paper and swallowing the package. People do this to hide the bitter taste. Abuse of oral amphetamines is not very common. First, it takes longer to feel the effects of the drugs when they are taken by mouth. Second, oral amphetamines do not produce an intense high. Third, more oral drug is needed to get the same effects you would get using other methods.

A second way of abusing amphetamines is by snorting them into the nose. When used this way, the drug reaches the brain faster than when amphetamines are

Linda, a drug addict, prepares to inject methamphetamine on November 30, 2005. At the time, she had been a meth user for many years and had been recently arrested. Since she started using the highly addictive drug, Linda has been put in jail more than 15 times. She has four children, three of whom are in foster care.

taken orally. A user will feel the effects of a snorted drug in about five minutes. Snorting amphetamines often causes intense burning in the nostrils. In fact, it can burn a hole right through a person's nose.

Some people dissolve amphetamines in water and inject the mixture into a vein with a needle. When the drug is used this way, it works within seconds, causing a powerful high and extreme pleasure. Methamphetamine that is smoked also causes these same feelings and effects. Most meth users prefer smoking the drug. They often use lightbulbs or pieces of glass as pipes.

LOSING SLEEP: SHORT-TERM EFFECTS

Amphetamines strengthen the signals that are sent between the brain and the body. This strengthening changes the way amphetamine users think, act, and feel. Amphetamines produce feelings of happiness, excitement, confidence, increased energy, alertness, and power. If these effects extend too far, however, an amphetamine user may experience **hallucinations**, in which he or she sees or hears things that are not really there. Amphetamines also cause headache, nervousness, jitteriness, and shakiness. Amphetamine users talk very quickly and have rapid eye movements. People using amphetamines also may experience a greater sex drive, do not feel hungry, and sleep very little. Amphetamines increase body temperature and heart rate. This can lead to excessive sweating, fast breathing, and an abnormal heartbeat.

IN TOO DEEP: LONG-TERM EFFECTS

When amphetamines are used for long periods of time, they cause many problems. Most of these problems are related directly to damage in the brain. Amphetamines prevent the body from making and using two neurotransmitters, dopamine and serotonin. These are important chemicals that help nerve cells "talk" to one another. Amphetamines also kill brain cells and cause certain parts of the brain to shrink. This can lead to mood changes and problems with thinking and memory. These changes can last a long time, even after the drug has been stopped. Sometimes, they last the rest of a person's life.

Amphetamine abusers can be confused, anxious, irritable, angry, or depressed. These feelings are made stronger by the users' not getting enough sleep and by intense **paranoia**, a type of **delusion** that causes

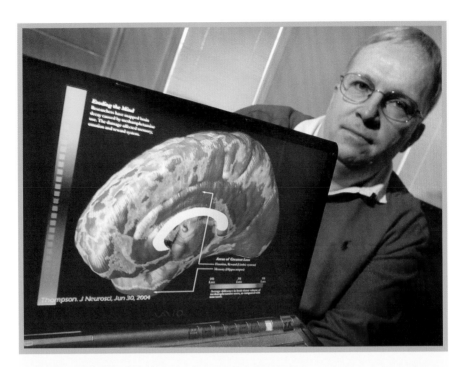

Methamphetamine abuse is a grave problem that can lead to serious health conditions, such as brain damage and memory loss. Dr. Jack Stump shows a PET scan of a methamphetamine user and the damage it can do to the brain.

people to believe falsely that other people want to hurt them. These strong feelings can lead to violent and unpredictable outbursts. For example, in 2006, a man in his early 20s got into a fight with someone who was high on crystal meth. The young man was doused in gasoline and set on fire.

Amphetamine abuse can shrink blood vessels. This makes it more difficult for the heart to move blood around the body. Eventually, the heart may stop working properly. Amphetamine use also can cause the heart to beat irregularly. These side effects increase a user's risk of having a heart attack or stroke.

THE AMPHETAMINE ROLLER COASTER

Although amphetamine abuse damages the body, amphetamines can have pleasurable and **reinforcing effects**. When users first start taking the drug, they

METH DIARIES

Below are real-life stories* of how meth has changed people's lives, as told by users and people who care about them.

FROM "ANONYMOUS":

I'm 14 years old, and I used meth for about three months. I never thought that it would destroy my life, but soon I was stealing money from my parents and shoplifting, often selling the things I stole to support my horrible habit. I was never at home. I was always lying to my parents. I was so violent. I didn't care about anything—even myself. The only thing that I cared about was meth. Then one night I started seeing and hearing and feeling things that weren't there—and I picked at my skin for hours. It was the most horrible feeling in the world. I thank God every day that my friend helped me quit.

FROM "MAMA":

My 20-year-old son passed away as a result of smoking meth. The ephedrine used to make meth opens up the sinuses, and it caused a hole to form in my son's nose. A common sinus infection spread to his brain, causing him to lose the use of the left side of his body. He was admitted to the hospital and placed in intensive care, where he was put on a ventilator [to help him breathe. He also] underwent brain and sinus surgery. Tests also showed he had

feel good. Soon, tolerance develops. People need to use more and more of the drug to get the same good feelings that they got the first time they took it. This often leads to "**bingeing**," in which people abuse large

severe, permanent lung damage. The doctors didn't expect him to make it. After 11 days he awoke and was taken off the ventilator and it looked like he was going to come home. Three days later, he pulled his knees to his chest and said he was having a panic attack and began vomiting blood. He died from a blood clot. Meth does kill.

FROM "JENN":

It was about three years ago when I first got introduced to "**ice**," or crystal meth. I had some friends visiting, and they brought the drug out. They kept [asking me to try it,] going on and on until I tried it. I did. I liked it. As time went by, I lost more and more weight. I got down to 89 pounds and looked like death. In the two-year time frame that I used meth, I lost my family's respect and a best friend thanks to a bad injection of the drug.

I stopped doing meth on September 20, 2004, and have been clean for almost two years. I am happier than I have ever been, but even after being clean this long I know that I could still easily give in to temptation. I still have headaches and even have the taste in my mouth, but I refuse to give in and start using again.

*These stories come from the Office of the Tennessee District Attorney and can be found at MethFreeTN.org.

amounts of the drug for days at a time. In many cases, people are so consumed by using drugs that they do not eat or sleep. "**Crashing**" happens at the end of a binge, when the user becomes too tired to continue.

AMPHETAMINE'S OTHER EFFECTS

Amphetamine abuse can drastically affect the way you look. It can cause your hair to fall out and your skin to become oily, which can lead to severe acne. Bingeing, not eating much, and eating unhealthy foods leads to extreme and unhealthy weight loss. Some people begin using meth to improve sexual pleasure, but in the long run, using meth can decrease sexual desire and the ability to have sex.

People who abuse amphetamines sometimes experience **amphetamine psychosis**. They lose touch with reality and the way they see, hear, and understand the world around them. People with amphetamine psychosis see and hear things that aren't real. They also often experience hallucinations and delusions—they see, hear, and believe things that are not true. An example of psychosis common in meth users is **delusional parasitosis**. People falsely believe that they are covered in bugs. People with delusional parasitosis will pick through their skin, sometimes right down to the bone, to get rid of the bugs.

When people are high, they may feel the need to repeat certain actions over and over again. This is called **tweaking**. The most common example of tweaking is when someone repeatedly takes apart and rebuilds an electronic device, such as a stereo or television.

Some of the most dangerous consequences of amphetamine abuse result from intravenous use (injection) of the drug. Street drugs are often "dirty." They contain impurities (or waste products) that are dangerous when

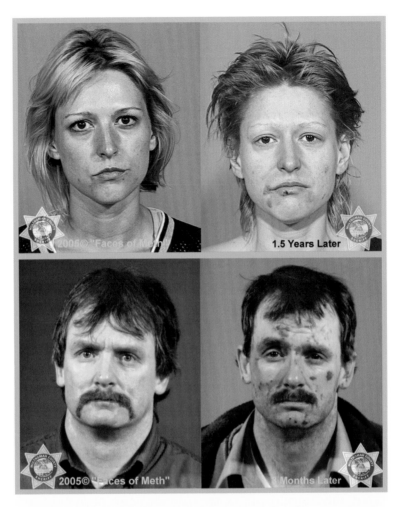

2005© "Faces of Meth"   1.5 Years Later

2005© "Faces of Meth"   3 Months Later

One of the many effects of methamphetamine use is an open sore, also known as a "meth sore" or "crank crater." Oftentimes, when users are high, they pick at their skin, which forms scabs that turn into scars. The apparent effects of this dangerous drug are displayed in the "before" and "after" police mug shots of these methamphetamine users.

injected. These impurities can plug up veins and stop blood from flowing. They can also be poisonous. For example, crystal meth that is not made properly may contain chemicals that can leak out through the veins into the skin and cause burns.

Users often share or reuse needles. This can spread infections. Bacterial infections are common and can be deadly. Endocarditis is an infection of the lining around the heart. It occurs when bacteria on a dirty needle enter the blood and travel to the heart.

Sharing needles also helps to spread blood-borne **diseases** such as Hepatitis C and HIV (the virus that causes AIDS). Also, because sexual excitement is heightened, people using amphetamines may have unprotected sex or sex with multiple partners. This increases the risk for spreading **sexually transmitted diseases (STDs)**, such as HIV, chlamydia, and gonorrhea.

Two common effects of meth use are "**meth mouth**" and "**speed bumps**." Meth mouth refers to serious tooth decay and bad breath. Sometimes, an abuser's teeth become so damaged that they either break off or have to be pulled. Some researchers believe that meth mouth happens because meth users don't eat healthy foods and don't brush their teeth. Others believe that the drug itself causes the problems.

Speed bumps are small red bumps or rashes. They often show up in places where meth has been injected, but they can be found anywhere on the body. They may be caused by impure drugs.

METH'S YOUNGEST VICTIMS

Amphetamines can seriously damage unborn children. If a woman takes amphetamines while she is pregnant, her baby can have birth defects, such as cleft palate (a hole in the roof of the mouth), small head size, eye problems, deformed arms and legs, and brain damage. If a woman uses these drugs near the end of her pregnancy, she may have her baby too soon, and it may be smaller than nor-

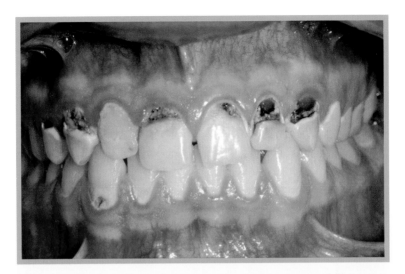

It is common for meth users to have dental hygiene problems and tooth decay, symptoms known as "meth mouth." There are many factors that contribute to the dental disease, such as long periods of poor oral hygiene, tooth grinding and clenching, and the drug's tendency to dry out saliva, which protects teeth against rotting. In addition, the corrosive ingredients found in methamphetamines can also contribute to dental decay.

mal. Babies born to women who use amphetamines may be cranky and restless. These babies can experience the same drug-**withdrawal** symptoms as an adult.

Amphetamines also can pass into breast milk in large enough amounts to affect the baby. This can result in poor feeding, restlessness, and crying. In 2002, a mother was arrested for the murder of her three-month-old son. He died from an overdose of methamphetamine that he received from her breast milk.

Growing up near a meth lab can affect children of any age. In 2003, four Oregon children between the ages of 4 and 15 were removed from a home where methamphetamine was being made. Three of the children had meth in their bloodstreams. This is not unusual for people who are exposed to this drug every day. They may swallow it accidentally, breathe in secondhand meth smoke, or absorb it through their skin. Individuals living in homes where meth is made also can be exposed to other dangerous chemicals that are used in its production. Children and teens are often removed from these homes and placed in protective custody.

METH LABS: CHEMICAL CENTRAL

Illegal methamphetamine is made in secret labs by people called "cooks." These labs can be found almost anywhere: homes, hotel rooms, garages, sheds, campgrounds, and even in the trunks of cars. Large labs, called "**superlabs**," can make more than 10 pounds (4.5 kg) of meth in 24 hours. Although the number of superlabs is growing, most labs that exist today are "**mom-and-pop labs**" that produce 1 to 2 ounces (30 to 60g) of meth each day.

Many of the chemicals used to make meth are dangerous. If the meth is not made properly, these chemicals can be left behind in the drug and can kill a user. These are some common ingredients used to make methamphetamine:

- Pseudoephedrine and ephedrine: Ingredients in cold remedies and herbal products
- Acetone: The main ingredient in nail-polish remover
- Toluene: A chemical used to make paint and paint thinner
- Iodine: A product used to disinfect (clean) wounds
- Anhydrous ammonia: A fertilizer
- Lithium: A chemical used in some batteries
- Lye: An ingredient in drain cleaner
- Camp stove fuel

An Indiana police officer holds a toy tanker filled with anhydrous ammonia, a nitrogen fertilizer used to make methamphetamine. The anhydrous ammonia is just one of the ingredients found in this home-made meth lab in Crawfordsville, Indiana. Meth labs are highly dangerous and illegal.

- Starter fluid
- Battery acid

Meth labs also produce large amounts of dangerous materials and gases. These are harmful to the people inside the lab, and to anyone close by. Some of the gases produced, such as phosphene gas, are odorless and colorless. However, they can kill a person if they are breathed in. Other gases, such as hydrogen gas, are explosive. Many meth labs are discovered only after they have exploded.

Chemicals used and produced in meth labs can seep into walls, carpet, and furniture. They can stay there for years, even after the meth lab is gone. Many buildings that contain meth labs must be torn down or decontaminated (cleaned and detoxified). In a meth lab, chemicals and by-products might be dumped down the sink or toilet, or thrown out with the garbage. This can contaminate water and soil, as well as sewers, ditches, and dumpsters.

Meth labs often are booby-trapped to stop or injure anyone who tries to come inside. Cooks are very protective of their product and are often users themselves. This makes them paranoid. They may set traps using fish-hooks, guns, or electrical or chemical barriers.

IS IT A METH LAB?

Most meth labs have similar features that give them away. Here are some of the signs law enforcement officials look for:

- Visitors and traffic at all hours (day and night)
- Paint-remover cans, pill packages, and broken glass in garbage cans
- Covered windows
- Propane tanks (with blue fittings)
- Unusual odors (anhydrous ammonia smells like cat urine)
- Coffee filters (with red residue on them)
- People who go outside to smoke

If you suspect someone has a meth lab, stay away and report it to a trusted adult or to law enforcement officials.

4

Legal Speed: Ritalin

Methylphenidate is an amphetamine-like stimulant. It is a powerful drug that can be habit forming if it is abused. Methylphenidate is available by prescription. It comes in different forms and strengths.

Ritalin was the first methylphenidate product, and it remains popular today for treating ADHD. Originally, Ritalin came as an immediate-release form. This form works quickly, and its effects last only a short time. Now, other forms of Ritalin exist that work for longer periods of time. Ritalin-SR is an intermediate-acting drug. Ritalin-LA works for longer periods of time. It works by releasing smaller amounts of medication throughout the day, so that it can be taken less often. It comes as a capsule that can be opened up so that the medication inside can be sprinkled on food or mixed into a drink. This makes swallowing the drug easier. **Metadate**, another longer-acting form of methylphenidate, can be used the same way.

Concerta is a tablet that contains methylphenidate in a paste. The paste is released through a tiny hole. This drug is taken once a day. **Methylin** is made as either a short- or intermediate-acting form of methylphenidate. The short-acting form is available as a liquid or a chewable tablet. The newest type of methylphenidate is a **transdermal patch system** called **Daytrana**. The patch is applied to the skin, and the drug in the patch is released into the skin. **Focalin** contains a drug called **dexmethylphenidate**. Its effects are almost the same as the other immediate-release methylphenidate-containing drugs. All of these drugs come in many different forms, strengths, sizes, colors, and shapes.

Even though these drugs are prescribed by doctors, they also can be found on the street. Immediate-release methylphenidate has the highest street value because it is the easiest to abuse. Drugs such as Concerta were designed to prevent abuse.

RITALIN KIDS: METHYLPHENIDATE'S USES

Methylphenidate is used most commonly to treat ADHD. In the past, doctors observed that methylphenidate had a calming effect on overactive children. This seemed odd, because stimulants are known to increase energy and excitement. Researchers began to ask how this could happen. At first, scientists thought that stimulant drugs would calm people down only if they had ADHD. The researchers believed that low doses could slow down the part of the brain responsible for hyperactivity.

This theory has since been proved wrong, but some people still believe it. New studies show that stimulants can help anyone to focus and concentrate, not just people with ADHD. The "calming" effects are just more obvious in people with ADHD.

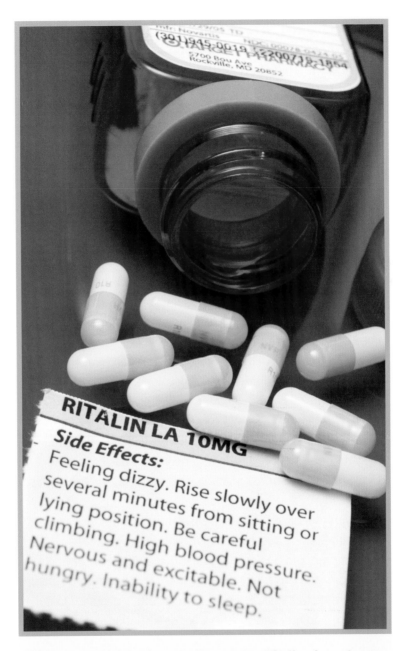

Doctors prescribe the stimulant drug, Ritalin, in order to treat ADHD. Ritalin is also commonly abused for its effects of loss of appetite, increased attention span, and the feeling of euphoria. Ritalin can be swallowed in a tablet form, crushed into a powder and snorted, or dissolved in water and injected. Ritalin abuse can lead to serious health problems.

METHYLPHENIDATE'S ABUSE POTENTIAL

When methylphenidate is used correctly, it is helpful and not often linked with addiction. However, when it is abused, methylphenidate causes effects similar to those of amphetamines. Methylphenidate abuse quickly increases the levels of dopamine, the brain chemical

WHAT IS ADHD?

Attention-deficit/hyperactivity disorder (ADHD) has been recognized as a medical condition since 1980. It has been challenging for doctors to develop guidelines for diagnosing ADHD, because the condition affects people in different ways. Diagnosing ADHD in young children can be difficult, because young children have not developed all of their communication skills. However, researchers now have a list of ADHD symptoms. If a child has enough of these symptoms in the right combination, he or she may have ADHD. The list of symptoms is published in an important book called the *Diagnostic and Statistical Manual of Mental Disorders*, which is currently in its fourth edition.

Symptoms of ADHD are classified into two major groups: attention deficits and hyperactivity/impulsivity.

Children and adults with ADHD have problems paying attention. It is especially hard for them to pay attention when there are distractions, such as noise or other people. Most children, parents, and teachers notice attention problems related to doing work at school or at home. A young person without ADHD may find it easy to sit down and finish his or her math homework in 30 minutes, but a person with ADHD might need several hours to finish the same homework. The young person with ADHD is constantly distracted.

that is responsible for feelings of pleasure. This makes people want to keep using the drug.

Methylphenidate is widely available and fairly easy to get. Many adults and young people have legal prescriptions. Some teenagers and college students abuse their own supply, or get methylphenidate from their

People use the word "hyperactive" a lot these days, but most young people act this way only occasionally. Young people who have ADHD often appear hyperactive and full of energy all the time. They often find it hard to sit still, and they may not listen when they are told to calm down and focus.

This hyperactivity is often associated with impulsive behavior. If someone is impulsive, he or she does things before thinking about what might happen next. A young person with ADHD might get into trouble with his or her parents or teachers because that young person does not think before he or she acts.

For a doctor to diagnose ADHD, symptoms must have lasted for at least six months, and must have started before a child reached the age of seven. The symptoms must affect a person's ability to act normally at school and with friends. Finally, the symptoms must be present when a person is in at least two different places, such as at home and at school.

Once parents, teachers, and doctors have had a chance to observe a young person's symptoms in that person's usual environment, they use a checklist to classify each case. Some people with ADHD have more difficulty focusing their attention. Others have more problems sitting still and thinking before they act.

friends. Methylphenidate also can be stolen from pharmacies.

HOW METHYLPHENIDATE IS USED

Methylphenidate can be taken by mouth, snorted, or injected. Taking it by mouth does not produce as much of a high as snorting it or injecting it. As a result, most people who abuse the drug do not use this method. Crushing and snorting methylphenidate produces a high similar to snorting cocaine. However, when methylphenidate is snorted and comes into contact with water, it forms an acid that can eat away at tissues and cartilage.

Injecting methylphenidate is risky. Prescription forms of methylphenidate contain other products that do not dissolve completely. When these substances are injected, they can clog veins and cause other harmful effects. As with other drugs that are injected, injecting methylphenidate can spread bacteria and viruses, including HIV.

REVVED UP ON RITALIN

Methylphenidate can cause headache, nervousness, shakiness, irritability, increased energy, alertness, trouble sleeping, upset stomach, loss of appetite, and weight loss. When used in low doses for the treatment of ADHD, methylphenidate also can cause tics, or unusual movements, and slow a person's growth. Under the advice of their doctor, many children who use methylphenidate will stop taking it for a few weeks or months at a time to help them grow normally. These breaks are called drug holidays.

Recently, methylphenidate has been linked with serious heart problems. These are caused by increases and changes in heart rate and blood pressure, and can lead to death.

Methylphenidate use also can cause seizures, hallucinations and delusions, depression, and suicidal thoughts.

THE RITALIN DEBATE

Since methylphenidate became popular, it has been at the center of a hot debate. Some researchers, parents, and teachers think it is a "miracle drug" that can help even the most overactive children calm down and focus. Other people believe that using methylphenidate is dangerous and leads to abusing other drugs and alcohol later in life. Some debaters go so far as to question whether ADHD is really a disease. Even celebrities have become involved. In 2005, actor Tom Cruise publicly criticized the use of Ritalin and other "psychiatric drugs." As a follower of Scientology, he was voicing the views held by many of the religion's followers who see Ritalin as a "chemical straitjacket" that does more harm than good.

In response to these debates, researchers started to study how the use of methylphenidate as a child related to the abuse of other drugs as an adult. Some evidence from the University of California, Berkeley, has shown a strong link. However, research from the National Institute on Drug Abuse has found that boys treated for ADHD with stimulant medications were less likely to abuse alcohol and drugs as adults, when compared with boys with ADHD who were not treated at all.

This debate has spread into the classroom. In past years, some teachers encouraged methylphenidate use in children with ADHD. A few schools even required children with ADHD to take the drug or not be allowed to stay in school. States now are passing laws to prevent principals and teachers from recommending the use of methylphenidate in children.

SPEEDING UP PRODUCTION

Legal use of methylphenidate has exploded in recent years. In the 1960s, very few people used the drug. By the 1970s, fewer than 200,000 children took the drug. After the ADHD guidelines were developed in 1980, more people began using methylphenidate. By 1990, 3 million people had prescriptions. By the year 2000, this number had jumped to 11 million.

The increase in methylphenidate use happened for other reasons besides the ADHD guidelines. Parents and teachers saw methylphenidate as an easy way to control children. The drug helped children to focus their attention and do better in school. Soon, methylphenidate was being given to children who probably did not need it. Use also increased because society as a whole became more accepting of the drug. (Still, when some children with ADHD become teenagers, they stop taking methylphenidate out of shame.) More adults also are being diagnosed with ADHD and started on methylphenidate. Finally, even though methylphenidate has been proved safe and effective only in children older than six, its use in younger children also is increasing.

More methylphenidate is used legally in the United States than in any other country. However, Canada and Australia also have seen sharp increases in the drug's use. Legal methylphenidate is used most commonly by people in white, middle- to upper-class families. Boys take methylphenidate more often than girls do.

5

The High Life: Dependence, Addiction, and Overdose

Drug use can lead to dependence. Dependence happens when a person's body becomes used to a drug and does not function as well without it. When this occurs, the person wants to keep using the drug. He or she has a hard time quitting because of unpleasant feelings known as withdrawal symptoms. Amphetamines and methylphenidate commonly cause dependence. People can become dependent on some of these drugs after using them only one time.

Even when these drugs are prescribed by a doctor and taken correctly, people can find it hard to stop using. People who take these drugs legally can experience some of the same withdrawal symptoms that are felt by people who abuse the drugs. Sometimes, when children with ADHD stop taking amphetamines or methylphenidate, they become depressed or feel as if they want to kill themselves. This happens if they stop taking the drug abruptly instead of decreasing their dose slowly.

Illegal use of amphetamines and methylphenidate causes a terrible and powerful withdrawal syndrome. The syndrome is even worse if the drugs have been smoked or injected. When people try to stop using these drugs, they have strong cravings for them. They also may feel depressed and anxious, and might feel like killing themselves. Some people become very tired and lose interest in the things they once enjoyed. Others become angry or aggressive. Drug withdrawal can also lead to paranoia, psychosis (losing touch with reality), hallucinations, and delusions. This withdrawal syndrome can last anywhere from a few days to several years. To prevent these feelings, people often go back to using the drug.

ADDICTION: HIGH STAKES

Addiction is a common and harmful effect of stimulant abuse. Addiction is a step beyond dependence. When a person is addicted to a drug, his or her dependence leads to reckless behaviors. These behaviors help the addict support his or her drug habit and get more drugs. Many addicts spend all of their money and lose their jobs. Some become homeless. Addicts may resort to stealing money or drugs. Some addicts may begin selling or manufacturing drugs. Addicts forge prescriptions, steal identities, write bad checks, and lie to their friends and families. Many addicts wind up in jail, or dead.

OVERDOSE: SITUATION CRITICAL

Overdose is a risk with any drug. However, it is less likely to occur with stimulants than it is with drugs

(continues on page 65)

THE SOCIAL CONSEQUENCES OF STIMULANT ABUSE

Every day, we see and hear more information about the harmful physical and mental health changes associated with drug use. Drug abuse takes a huge toll on our society and our economy. As abuse increases, people become less productive at work and at school. Drug abuse also increases the costs of health care and law enforcement. Drug abuse also can destroy families and relationships. This sad cost of drug abuse is often hidden from the public eye.

SCHOOL AND WORK

- Drug abusers are more likely to die young. They also are more likely to get so sick or injured that they can no longer work.
- Drug abusers who have jobs cost their bosses twice as much (in medical and workers' compensation claims) as nonusers do.
- Drug use is associated with fewer job opportunities and lower wages.
- Drug users focus on getting and using drugs. This means that they usually do not do well at work or at school.
- Drug users tend to experience memory loss. They also have problems with abstract thinking. This makes it hard for them to learn and do their jobs.

HEALTH CARE

- Health care represents the largest direct cost of drug abuse for society.
- In the United States, hospitalizations due to drug use increased by more than 30% between 1988 and 1995.

(continues on page 64)

(continued from page 63)

- People on drugs are more likely to have certain illnesses that are expensive to treat.
- The treatments to help abusers stop taking drugs are very expensive.

CRIME

- People may be more likely to commit crimes when they are high on drugs. Drugs make people do things without thinking about what might happen. They also are less afraid of being caught.
- Drug users commit crimes to get drugs or money.
- Millions of dollars are spent on police, legal, and corrections services related to drug use.
- Drug trafficking is closely tied with organized crime groups whose members manufacture, sell, and use drugs. These groups often use violence to stop other gangs or law enforcement agencies from cutting into their profits.

FAMILIES AND RELATIONSHIPS

- Drug abuse is more likely than poverty to destroy families.
- Family members of drug abusers may become victims of drug-related theft, violence, and sexual crimes.
- Families of drug abusers are at much higher risk for abuse and neglect.
- Women, children, older adults, and people with disabilities are the most common victims of drug-related crimes and abuse.

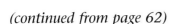

(continued from page 62)

such as heroin. This is because stimulant users quickly develop a tolerance to the drug.

The amount of a drug that causes an overdose is different for everyone. Whether a person will overdose depends on how used to the drug they have become and how strong the drug is. Drugs such as crystal meth, which are manufactured on the street, are more dangerous than drugs made by drug companies. This is because street drugs have different ingredients and strengths, depending on how they were made.

The risk of overdose is higher if a drug is injected. This is because the drug goes directly into the bloodstream and doesn't go through the kidneys and liver. These organs help to make drugs less harmful.

A stimulant overdose can cause sweating, increased blood pressure, a faster heart rate and breathing rate, and enlarged pupils (the small, dark opening in the center of each eye). A stimulant overdose also can lead to agitation, anger, and violent outbursts. Confusion, delusions, hallucinations, and psychosis are common. Body temperature can go up, which may lead to dehydration. Overdose also can cause seizures, heart attack, stroke, kidney failure, swelling of the brain or lungs, coma, and death.

Overdose can become serious very quickly. If an overdose is suspected, the affected person should be taken to the hospital as soon as possible. Those who are with the person should not stop to worry about whether they or the person with the overdose might get into trouble. The sooner the person gets medical treatment, the more likely it is that he or she will live and not suffer any permanent damage.

When a stimulant overdose victim is taken to the hospital, he or she may be put into an ice bath designed to lower body temperature. The victim also may be

(continues on page 68)

THE WORD ON THE STREET

Street names and slang terms are often used to refer to drugs of abuse and the people who use them. The following is a list of some commonly used terms. Although this list is long, it does not include all of the terms. Street names and slang terms vary by region, by state, or even by city, and they are always changing.

RITALIN'S STREET NAMES
Jif, Kibbles and Bits, kiddy cocaine, MPH, pineapple, Rball, Rids, Rit, Skippy, smart drug, Smarties, uppers, vitamin R, West Coast

Ritalin is often combined with **Talwin** (a prescription painkiller). This combination produces a high very similar to the high produced when cocaine or methamphetamine is mixed with heroin. The Ritalin/Talwin combination is referred to as poor man's heroin, crackers, one and ones, Ts and Rs, Ts and Rits, or Rits and Ts.

METHAMPHETAMINE'S STREET NAMES
bathtub crank, Batu, Bennies, biker's coffee, blade, blue devils, boo, bumps, chalk, chicken feed, Christina, Christmas tree meth, crank, crink, Cristy, crypto, crystal, crystal meth, gak, glass, go, jib, ice, meth, motorcycle crack, Nazi dope, OZs, pink elephants, poor man's cocaine, redneck cocaine, rip, rock, Scooby snax, Scootie, sparkle, speed, spoosh, tick tick, Tina, trash, tweak, white cross, wash, ya ba, zip, zoom

TERMS USED TO DESCRIBE THE FEELING OF INTOXICATION
amping, amped, buzzed, cranked up, foiled, fried, gakked, gassing, geeked, geeking, gurped, heated, high, jacked,

lit, ripped, pissed, pumped, red, rolling, rolling hard, scattered, sketching, speeding, sparked, spracked, spun, spun monkey, stoked, talkie, twacked, tweaking, tweaked, twisted, wacked, wide awake, wide open, wired, worked, zoomin'

WORDS USED TO DESCRIBE METH USERS

basehead, battery bender, clucker, crackhead, crackie, crankhead, crankster, fiend, gangster, geek, geeker, geeter, go go loser, meth fiend, meth head, meth monster, shadow person, sketch monster, speed freak, spin doctor, spinster, tweaker, wigger

METH LAB SLANG

Box lab: A small, moveable meth lab

Cook or cooker: A person who makes meth

Cooking class: Teaching someone to make meth

Mom-and-pop lab: A smaller and more common type of meth lab

Superlab: A large lab that can produce 10 pounds (4.5 kg) of meth in 24 hours

RELATED LAB TERMS

Elbow: One pound (16 ounces or 0.45 kg)

Eightball: One-eighth of an ounce (3.5 g)

Gram: 0.035 ounces

Half elbow: One-half pound (8 ounces or 0.23 kg)

Ounce: 0.0625 lbs (28.35 g)

Paper: 0.0035 ounces (one-tenth of a gram) or less

(continues on page 68)

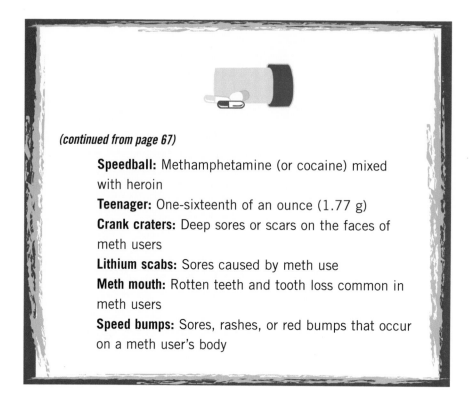

(continued from page 67)

Speedball: Methamphetamine (or cocaine) mixed with heroin

Teenager: One-sixteenth of an ounce (1.77 g)

Crank craters: Deep sores or scars on the faces of meth users

Lithium scabs: Sores caused by meth use

Meth mouth: Rotten teeth and tooth loss common in meth users

Speed bumps: Sores, rashes, or red bumps that occur on a meth user's body

(continued from page 65)

placed in a dark, quiet room to reduce agitation, aggression, and anxiety. Overdose victims also may be given medicines that will prevent seizures, bring down blood pressure, and stop hallucinations and delusions.

6

Who Uses Stimulants and Why They Do It

Illegal use of stimulant drugs is widespread and affects many parts of modern society. There is little information available about the abuse of methylphenidate because agencies have only been collecting national data for about six years. Although methylphenidate abuse remains a problem, results from a U.S. study called "Monitoring the Future" show an overall decrease in use by high school students. That same study, which examined drug use data from 2001 to 2003, suggested that the number of adults taking this drug has remained the same. Another important study, the National Survey on Drug Use and Health (NSDUH), showed a very slight decrease in use across all ages in the United States. Information from the Drug Abuse Warning Network shows that the number of people being treated in U.S. emergency departments has also been decreasing since 1995. Similar results have been seen in Canada.

METHAMPHETAMINE TRENDS

Illegal use and production of methamphetamine continues to be a major concern. According to the NSDUH, in 2003, about 1.3 million Americans 12 years of age and older used methamphetamine. The same survey showed that 10.4 million people have used meth in their lifetimes. Rates of use by teenagers in some states and Canadian provinces seem to be leveling off or decreasing. However, this change is often balanced out by increases in other groups.

Abuse of methamphetamine began in California and other Western states. It continues to spread eastward. As meth becomes widely available in more parts of the country, experts predict that more people will use it.

More law enforcement agencies are recognizing meth as their biggest drug threat. They say it is a bigger problem than cocaine and heroin. The National Drug Threat Survey has shown that methamphetamine-related crimes have risen. Also, in many parts of the country, more people are being arrested for making or selling meth. More people also are being treated for meth addiction. The costs related to cleaning up meth labs went from $2 million in 1995 to $16.2 million in 2003.

A new trend related to methamphetamine is a decrease in use of the powdered drug in favor of "ice," a more pure form. When law enforcement officials tightened rules surrounding meth production, the number of U.S.-based labs decreased sharply. As a result, more methamphetamine was smuggled in from Mexico. In Mexico, it is easier to get the ingredients to make large

The crystalline form of methamphetamine is an extremely pure form of the drug that may cause longer lasting and much more intense effects. Crystal meth can cause erratic, violent behavior, suppressed appetite, interference in sleeping behavior, tremors and convulsions, increased blood pressure, and an irregular heart rate. It is highly addictive.

amounts of methamphetamine. Mexican labs are usually bigger, and their "cooks" are well trained to produce ice. Like the spread of powdered meth, the spread of ice started in the West and moved eastward.

METHYLPHENIDATE USERS

Many different groups of people abuse stimulants. Methylphenidate is most widely abused by high school and college students. However, rates of use are quite low when compared with other drugs such as Ecstasy and marijuana. Methylphenidate is also sometimes mixed with Talwin to produce heroin-like effects. This combination is used more often by certain groups, such as prostitutes and people with lower incomes. Finally, there have been a few reports of teachers and nurses stealing methylphenidate from their students or patients.

Methamphetamine, like methylphenidate, often is abused by teenagers and young adults. But meth use has reached almost every part of society. Widespread

THE HIGH PRICE OF STIMULANT USE

The street price of a stimulant depends on:

- What kind of stimulant it is
- Where it is purchased
- How pure it is
- How much is available

COCAINE

Cocaine is available in two common forms. Crack cocaine typically sells for about $110 per gram (0.035 ounces) in the United States and Canada. In other countries, such as Venezuela, it sells for only a dollar or two per gram. The second form of cocaine is more pure then crack cocaine. In the United States a gram of cocaine powder costs about $110. In Canada the price is typically around $59.80.

Cocaine may be purchased in smaller quantities. Crack is often sold in 0.1 to 0.2 gram dosages that are called "rocks".

These rocks range in price from about $10 to $25 in the United States and Canada.

use began in the rave and dance scene, and within gay communities. Soon, meth was being abused by sex-trade workers and homeless people. People of all education and income levels now take meth. It is particularly popular among young girls and street youth. In the United

ECSTASY

Ecstasy costs about $25 a tablet in the United States and $8 in Canada. However, the typical price of a tablet can be as low as $3 (in the Dominican Republic) and as high as $100 (in Southeast Asia).

RITALIN

The street price of Ritalin is less variable than the prices of some other stimulants. In Canada and the United States, Ritalin typically sells for around $5 a tablet. When Ritalin and Talwin are sold together, the price increases to about $25.

METHAMPHETAMINE

One gram of methamphetamine typically costs about $97 in the United States and $75 in Canada. In some parts of Africa and Asia, methamphetamine costs only $1 per gram. On the other hand, in Japan, methamphetamine typically sells for almost $650 per gram.

Like cocaine, methamphetamine also can be bought in smaller amounts. A "paper" contains about 0.1 grams of methamphetamine and costs around $10 in the United States and $8 in Canada.

States, methamphetamine use is highest among white and Hispanic people. It is also more common in towns and rural communities than it is in cities.

DRUGS IN DISGUISE

Sometimes, people become stimulant users without intending to. Drug dealers commonly mix methamphetamine with other drugs, such as Ecstasy, marijuana, heroin, and ketamine. They do this to increase their profits or hook new users. Methylphenidate is often mixed with baking soda and disguised as cocaine.

REASONS FOR USE

There are many reasons why people abuse drugs. High school and college students use methylphenidate to focus and stay awake so that they can study. They also use it as a party drug. Methylphenidate produces the same sort of high as cocaine, but the high lasts longer and the drug costs less. The methylphenidate/Talwin combination is used as an alternative to heroin, which is more expensive.

People often use methamphetamine to give them extra energy. This helps them to work harder and get more done. People involved in the rave scene take methamphetamine because its long-lasting effects allow them to party all night long. Homosexual males use it to make sex better. Prostitutes, homeless people, and street youth take methamphetamine to decrease their needs for food, sleep, and shelter. The drug also allows them to "escape" from the reality of their lives. Young girls use methamphetamine to lose weight. Some people also use it to **self-treat** illnesses such as asthma, depression, and ADHD.

Peer pressure is another powerful reason for drug use. People, especially teenagers, often feel as if they need

(continues on page 76)

THE MYTH OF THE METH DIET

In our current world of stick-thin fashion models and clothes that come in size 00, the pressure to be thin is on the minds of many young people. The truth, however, is that everyone's body is different, and not everyone is meant to be a size 00. A person's size does not matter if that person is healthy and happy. It also takes time and effort to lose weight in a healthy way. But because society pressures them to be thin, some young people turn to methamphetamine use as an "easy" way to lose weight.

When a person uses methamphetamine, he or she does not feel hungry. A user on a meth binge may not eat or sleep for days at a time. Yet, this lack of nutrition is dangerous and takes a toll on the body. If someone starves his or her body's organs for too long, the organs shut down. Because the teenage body is still growing and developing, the risks associated with not eating properly are particularly dangerous to a teenager.

When a person stops using meth, his or her appetite comes back stronger than it was before. As a result, such a person often will overeat to restore lost nutrients and energy. This behavior sets up a cycle of starvation and overeating that is stressful and damaging. Such a cycle makes it difficult for the body to function normally. In the end, a person who uses meth for weight loss may end up weighing more than he or she did before turning to meth.

The effects of starvation not only affect the internal parts of the body, but also can cause disturbing visible changes. These include hair loss, skin rashes, and slower

(continues on page 76)

(continued from page 75)

Methamphetamine use is known to cause extreme weight loss, which is why it has become a drug of choice for people seeking weight loss alternatives. This before-and-after mug shot shows a meth user who unintentionally lost a good deal of weight while using the drug, as noted by his sunken cheeks.

healing of wounds. Meth use also can lead to tooth decay, acne, and other skin problems. A person who uses meth to improve his or her appearance often ends up looking much worse than before the start of the "meth diet."

(continued from page 74)

to do drugs to fit in with their friends. Some teens take drugs because of boredom. Others do it to escape from bad family situations. Still others try drugs to see what it feels like, or because it makes them seem grown up.

You may think everyone around you is using stimulants, but this is far from the truth. Many people choose not to do drugs at all. At first, drugs may make you feel better and look important. But long-term drug use leads to fewer friends, bad changes in appearance, poor grades, and less money. Drug use also may lead to a criminal record, or even to death. You are not alone if you say no to drugs.

Policing
Stimulants

Drug laws differ from country to country. Even the United States and Canada, which share a border, handle illegal drugs differently.

LAWS IN THE UNITED STATES
In the United States, the Drug Enforcement Administration (DEA), local and state police, and other agencies—such as the Federal Bureau of Investigation (FBI)—are responsible for drug control. These groups follow laws set out in the federal government's "Controlled Substances Act" (CSA). This act groups drugs into **schedules**, or categories. A drug's schedule is based on how dangerous the drug is, how likely it is to be abused, and its medical uses.

A DEA agent and a police chief gather toxic material during a methamphetamine lab bust in Damascus, Virginia, in 2004. The Drug Enforcement Agency is in charge of controlling drug use in the United States.

Schedule I drugs have a high potential for abuse and are very dangerous. They have no medical use in the United States. Ecstasy and heroin are Schedule I drugs.

Schedule II drugs have a high abuse potential, but are used to treat a limited number of medical conditions. These drugs include methylphenidate, cocaine, and amphetamine (including methamphetamine).

Schedule III drugs are less likely to lead to dependence than those in Schedules I and II. Tylenol with codeine is a Schedule III drug. Schedule IV drugs (such as Talwin) and Schedule V drugs (such as cough medicines with codeine) have a lower abuse potential. Drugs in Schedules III, IV, and V are commonly used in medicine.

NORTH AMERICA'S MOST WANTED STIMULANTS

There are many types of stimulants. Some are mild and some are toxic. Some are legal and others are illegal. Some help to treat illness and some cause illness. Here are some of the most commonly used stimulants.

LEGAL STIMULANTS
- Caffeine (in chocolate, energy drinks, and some sodas)
- Nicotine (in cigarettes and chewing tobacco)
- Pseudoephedrine (in Sudafed and other common cold and flu products)
- Ephedrine
- Ephedra
- Stimulant laxatives, such as bisacodyl and sennosides
- Sibutramine (Meridia)
- Methylphenidate (Ritalin, Metadate, and Concerta)
- Amphetamines and Dextroamphetamine (Adderall, Dexedrine, and Dextrostat)

CANADIAN LAWS

In Canada, the Royal Canadian Mounted Police works with local and provincial law enforcement to control the sale and use of drugs. Canada has eight drug schedules (categories) outlined in its "Controlled Drugs and Substances Act" (CDSA). Schedules I through V include

- Methamphetamine (Desoxyn)

Some of these stimulants are legal drugs only when used correctly and prescribed by a doctor or purchased from a drugstore or pharmacy. If these drugs are used improperly, abused, sold illegally, or used to manufacture other drugs, they are no longer considered legal.

Caffeine and nicotine can be bought and/or consumed in large or unlimited amounts. There are laws against selling nicotine products to people until they reach a certain age. This age is 18 in most U.S. states and Canadian provinces, but some states and provinces have upped the age to 19.

ILLEGAL STIMULANTS
- Ecstasy (MDMA)
- Cocaine and crack
- Crystal meth or ice (methamphetamine that is not made by legitimate drug companies)

all drugs of abuse. The most dangerous and highly addictive drugs, such as methamphetamine, are in Schedule I. As the schedule number increases, the risk of abuse and dangers go down. Marijuana is an example of a Schedule II drug. Schedule III includes all of the other amphetamines and methylphenidate. Schedules VI and VII include chemicals and certain drugs, such as pseudoephedrine and ephedrine, which are used to make illegal methamphetamine.

MISTAKES, MISHAPS AND MISDEMEANORS

Punishments in the United States

In the United States, it is against the law for someone to have a **controlled substance** without a valid reason. Fines for **possession** of one of these drugs are at least $1,000, and a convicted person may also face prison time of up to three years. Punishments are harsher if a person is convicted of trafficking (selling) drugs. Methamphetamine traffickers face up to $20 million in fines and a lifetime in prison. Methylphenidate and other amphetamine traffickers can face up to 30 years in prison and up to $10 million in fines. **Importing** or **exporting** controlled substances also leads to steep penalties. People may be fined up to $20 million and face five years to life in prison. Manufacturing drugs leads to prison sentences as long as 20 years and fines of up to $2 million.

Canadian Punishments

In Canada, no one may possess any drugs in Schedules I to IV of the CDSA except for valid reasons and legal purposes. Anyone found possessing methamphetamine faces a minimum of a $1,000 fine and up to seven years in prison. People found with other amphetamines or

TOYS TAKE PART IN DRUG BUST

A Colorado investigation started in September 2005 and ended when 21 members of a methamphetamine distribution ring were charged with drug possession and trafficking. The members of the ring faced 10 years to life in prison if convicted.

During their investigations, the DEA and the police seized over 45 pounds (20 kg) of ice (a pure form of methamphetamine), 2.4 pounds (1.1 kg) of cocaine, $59,000

(continues on page 84)

DEA Agent Jeffrey Sweetin holds a replica of a Sesame Street Elmo doll that was used to smuggle 4 pounds of methamphetamine from California to Colorado in 2006. Drug smugglers will use any way possible to secretly transport their drugs, from having someone swallow large quantities to hiding the drug in a children's toy.

(continued from page 83)

in cash and a Sesame Street Elmo doll. Elmo was taken because the investigating officers found 4 pounds (1.8 kg) of methamphetamine hidden inside.

To avoid getting caught, drug traffickers often come up with original and inventive schemes. "They will use anything, including children's toys, to hide their illegal drugs from authorities," Attorney Troy Eid said in a press release issued by the DEA.

Interesting Fact: 45 pounds (20 kg) of meth is about 4 million doses, and is worth more than $860,000 (whole-sale) or around $2 million dollars on the street.

with methylphenidate face a $1,000 fine and up to three years in prison. The punishments for trafficking, importing and exporting, and manufacturing drugs are more severe. Prison sentences range from up to 10 years for amphetamines (excluding methamphetamine) and methylphenidate to life for methamphetamine.

8

Getting Help

People who abuse stimulants often appear excited and energetic at first. They may get a lot of work done and they may seem happier than normal. However, as use continues, this begins to change. Are you one of those people? If you are, your friends and family members may notice differences in the way you look and act.

Changes in a user's appearance may include weight loss, hair loss, acne, tooth rot, skin infections and rashes, bad breath and dry mouth, dilated (enlarged) pupils, bloodshot eyes, and heavy sweating. Depending on the way a person is using a drug, he or she may develop a bleeding nose, **track marks**, or a cough that does not go away. Some users experience tremors (shakes) and seizures.

Changes in a drug user's behavior also are common. Stimulant users often lose interest in eating and sleeping. They may become hyperactive, angry, or aggressive. They may seem depressed, and lose interest in doing things that they used to like to do. Abusers often become paranoid and may lose touch with reality. Additionally, they may begin to neglect their appearance and forget to do simple things such as showering.

Users also begin to withdraw from their families and friends. They may isolate themselves or start hanging around new people who are destructive. Stimulant abusers often skip class or work. They do poorly in their studies and may be fired from their jobs. They lie about everything, including where they have been and with whom they are spending time. People abusing drugs also keep secrets. They may begin borrowing money or stealing to buy drugs. Some people sell personal items, such as stereos.

Users may carry **drug paraphernalia** with them, or may keep paraphernalia in their homes or cars. Drug paraphernalia may include broken lightbulbs and simple pipes, both of which are used to smoke drugs. People who snort drugs often have razor blades, mirrors, and straws. Injection users may have rubber tubing, needles, and spoons. Some drug users also may carry small plastic bags, balloons, or condoms.

WHERE TO GET HELP

If someone starts using and abusing drugs and begins to plan his or her life around them, that person has a problem that is serious and will get worse. If you are that person, you must get help immediately. As a first step, talk to a trustworthy adult. Go to any adult with whom you feel comfortable who will be understanding and

A lightbulb can be used as drug paraphernalia, particularly for meth-amphetamine use. The powder or crystal is placed in a bulb that has been cleared inside. A lighter is then used to heat the bulb and the user inhales the smoke from it. This lightbulb, which was found during a police search, has a pen inserted through the socket, which was used to inhale the methamphetamine.

nonjudgmental. Examples of such adults might include teachers, counselors, parents, family friends, or doctors. Treatment centers also have trained staff members who can help you.

You should not worry about getting into trouble. Seeking help and getting clean are your most important tasks. You will find that most people will support you in your efforts and will be proud of you for taking action.

There are many treatments available for stimulant addiction. Some treatments involve both medicines and

Ricky, a meth user, was severely burned in 2004 when his meth lab exploded as he was cooking a new batch. More than 40% of his body was burned in the accident and he is still struggling with the pain. The large number of methamphetamine laboratories is a result of the growing popularity of the drug, which has led an overall increase in the number of burn victims across the country.

drug counseling. Antidepressant medications help to treat depression. They also can decrease a person's cravings and the reinforcing effects of the drug. Occasionally, doctors will give antipsychotic medications to drug abusers. These medications help to stop hallucinations and delusions.

Drug counseling remains the most important part of treatment. Counseling helps people to change the way they think about drugs. Counseling programs help people to feel better about themselves and to deal with stress. The programs also help abusers to avoid drugs in the future if they find themselves in places where drugs are being offered. Some programs involve following guidelines that are set out in a manual. Other programs assign a caseworker to each person to help that person manage his or her addiction.

Longer treatments—in which a person lives at a treatment center—have been shown to be more successful than some other forms of treatment. But many people who abuse drugs cannot afford this type of "sleepaway" treatment. They usually attend treatment sessions during the day and then go home at night. Many of these people find it hard to resist using drugs when they are away from a program.

For any treatment program to be successful, a drug user has to want to be a part of it. Also, an abuser must make a conscious effort to avoid places and situations where there might be drugs. Counselors encourage users to find new activities that will keep them happy and occupied. It also is important for a user to surround himself or herself with friends who are drug free and who encourage the recovering abuser to stay drug free.

Information about treatment centers in the United States can be found on the Substance Abuse and Mental Health Services Administration (SAMHSA) Web site

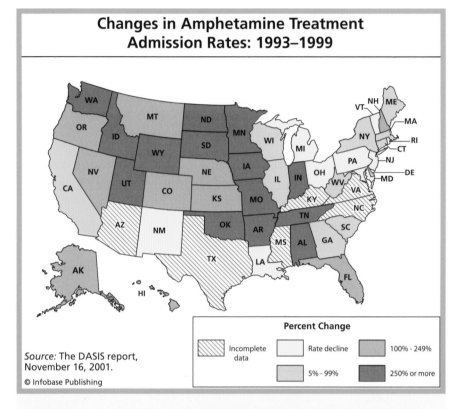

Changes in Amphetamine Treatment Admission Rates: 1993–1999

Percent Change

Incomplete data	Rate decline	100% - 249%
	5% - 99%	250% or more

Source: The DASIS report, November 16, 2001.

© Infobase Publishing

A growing number of people are getting help for amphetamine abuse. Amphetamine treatment admission rates increased between 1993 and 1999 by 250% or more in 14 U.S. states and by 100% to 249% in 10 other states.

(http://dasis3.samhsa.gov/Default.aspx).Information about treatment centers in Canada can be found on the Canadian Centre on Substance Abuse (CCSA) Web site (http://www.ccsa.ca/CCSA/EN/Addiction_Databases/ TreatmentServicesForm.htm).

IF A FRIEND OR PARENT IS USING STIMULANTS...

When someone you know is abusing stimulants, remember that your safety comes first. If you are in a bad situ-

GETTING HELP: 12-STEP PROGRAMS

Narcotics Anonymous (NA) is an international, nonprofit organization that helps people who want to stop using drugs. Anyone who has an addiction to drugs can become a member of the program.

NA offers a 12-step program similar to the alcohol-treatment program developed by Alcoholics Anonymous (AA). NA focuses on providing members with a support network that involves other users. The organization also encourages spirituality and complete **abstinence** from addictive substances. Some of NA's central principles are as follows:

- A person must be able to admit that he or she has a problem.
- The person must seek help for the problem.
- The person must evaluate himself or herself and his or her actions.
- The person must try to make up for any mistakes that he or she has made.
- The person must try to help others who are facing drug addiction.

NA focuses on facing life one day at a time. NA does not employ counselors or doctors. The success of the program depends on addicts sharing their experiences and helping other addicts.

(continues on page 92)

(continued from page 91)

Crystal Meth Anonymous (CMA) is a relatively new organization. It is geared toward people who are addicted to crystal methamphetamine. The group has branches in the United States, Canada, New Zealand, and Australia. CMA is a 12-step program adapted from AA, and it relies on the same principles as NA.

For more information about these programs or to find a meeting near you, visit the following Web sites:

Narcotics Anonymous: http://www.na.org/
Crystal Meth Anonymous: http://www.crystalmeth.org/

ation, leave. When this is not possible, call your local police or 911. Even if your safety is not threatened, it is still important to get help. Talk to a trusted adult.

You can help people addicted to stimulants by being supportive and encouraging. Try not judge them or their actions. If they decide to seek help, you can be supportive by attending meetings with them if they do not want to go alone. And remember: It is important not to bring up a person's drug abuse when that person is high, violent, or angry. This will only make the situation worse. When you find a good time to talk, tell your addicted friends or family members that you care about them, but their drug abuse is affecting everyone around them.

(continues on page 96)

FAST FACTS ABOUT STIMULANTS

Drugs of abuse are a reality in our society. However, the more we know about them the easier they are to refuse. Some important facts that everyone should know about stimulants are as follows:

STIMULANTS

- Stimulants can be highly addictive and dangerous substances.
- They work by increasing the levels of chemical signalers in the brain.
- Stimulants cause excitement, euphoria, energy, headache, and jitteriness; they also cause decreased appetite and decrease the need for sleep.
- Stimulants cause high blood pressure, increased heart rate, seizures, heart attack, strokes, and psychosis.
- Stimulants come in many different forms, shapes, sizes, colors, and strengths.
- Caffeine, nicotine, cocaine, Ecstasy, amphetamines, and methylphenidate are all stimulants.
- Stimulants exist in both legal and illegal forms.
- People use stimulants to help them study, to party, to escape from reality, to make sex better, to lose weight, and because of peer pressure.

AMPHETAMINES

- Amphetamines are used legally to treat ADHD and narcolepsy.
- Amphetamines include Adderall, Dexedrine, Dextrostat, and methamphetamine.

(continues on page 94)

(continued from page 93)

- People abuse amphetamines orally and by snorting, smoking, or injecting them.
- Amphetamines cause acne, hair loss, bad teeth, rashes, and impotence. Injecting drugs can spread diseases.
- Methamphetamine lasts longer in the body than any other stimulant.
- Dealers disguise methamphetamine by mixing it into other drugs.
- Methamphetamine is made in secret labs.
- Meth labs can be explosive. They produce many harmful chemicals. They also may be booby-trapped.
- Illegally made drugs are more dangerous than legal drugs because the illegal drugs contain impurities.

METHYLPHENIDATE

- Methylphenidate is an amphetamine-like stimulant with effects similar to cocaine.
- Methylphenidate is another name for Ritalin, Metadate, Concerta, and Methylin.
- It is used legally to treat ADHD and narcolepsy.
- Methylphenidate often is abused by high school and college students.
- Methylphenidate is taken by mouth, snorted, or injected.
- Legal use of methylphenidate has increased; illegal use of methylphenidate has decreased.

- Legal methylphenidate is commonly used by boys in white, middle-class families.

DEPENDENCE, ADDICTION, OVERDOSE, AND TREATMENT

- Legal and illegal use of stimulants can lead to dependence. Dependence happens when a person becomes used to a drug and does not function well without it.
- Withdrawal causes unpleasant effects, including depression.
- Overdose victims need immediate medical attention because their condition may worsen quickly.
- Signs of stimulant abuse include enlarged pupils, tooth rot, skin infections, track marks, tremors, anger, hyperactivity, and paranoia.
- Stimulant abuse causes people to withdraw from family and friends, skip class or work, or steal.
- Stimulant abuse is a serious matter. If you are abusing stimulants, you must get help immediately.
- Talk to a trusted adult if you are worried about yourself or someone else abusing stimulants.
- Many treatment programs are available.

PUNISHMENTS

- Punishments for using, dealing, making, and importing or exporting drugs are strict. People convicted of such crimes face heavy fines and life in prison.

(continued from page 92)

Stimulants are dangerous and highly addictive drugs, but help is available for people who want to give up their drug habit. If you or someone you know is using stimulants, remember that you are not alone. Getting help as soon as possible is the best way to make sure that drugs do not destroy lives.

GLOSSARY

Abstinence The act of choosing not to participate in a certain activity, such as taking drugs.

Addiction A compulsive need for and use of habit-forming substances, even when the user knows they are harmful. It is often associated with reckless behaviors such as stealing and lying.

ADD *See* "Attention Deficit Disorder."

Adderall A stimulant drug that is commonly used to treat ADHD. It contains mixed amphetamine salts. It can be dangerous and deadly if it is abused.

ADHD *See* "Attention-Deficit/Hyperactivity Disorder"

Amphetamine psychosis A psychosis that is caused by amphetamine abuse. *See* "Psychosis."

Amphetamines A class of highly addictive and dangerous drugs. Amphetamines come in legal (Dexedrine) and illegal (crystal meth) forms. Legally, amphetamines are used to treat narcolepsy and ADHD. Illegal use can lead to paranoia, hallucinations, and death.

Attention deficit disorder (ADD) The original name for a group of symptoms associated with problems focusing and difficulty concentrating. ADD was classified as a medical condition in 1980.

Attention-deficit/hyperactivity disorder (ADHD) The more recent name for ADD. This definition also includes symptoms of hyperactivity and impulsivity. The change to the definition was made in 1987.

Axons Single, long nerve fibers that allow neurons to send messages and thus communicate with one another.

Bingeing Using drugs for many days at a time without stopping to eat or sleep. Bingeing often leads to **"crashing."**

Blood-borne diseases Diseases spread through blood or other body fluids. Injecting drugs is a common way to spread these diseases. Hepatitis C and HIV are blood-borne diseases.

Caffeine   A mild stimulant commonly found in chocolate and some soda drinks. Caffeine is not usually dangerous, unless it is consumed in very large amounts.

Cell body   The part of a neuron that contains the nucleus. The cell body controls the actions of a neuron.

Central effects   Effects on the body that happen because of changes in the levels of chemical signalers in the brain. Central effects may alter the way a person feels, acts, or thinks.

Chemical messengers   *See* "Neurotransmitters."

Clandestine labs   Secret locations where illegal drugs are made. Crystal meth and Ecstasy are produced in clandestine labs. These labs are very dangerous. Besides producing illegal drugs, they also produce poisonous and explosive chemicals.

Cocaine   An illegal stimulant drug that is short acting and highly addictive. It is widely abused.

Concerta   A drug used to treat ADHD. It consists of a capsule containing a paste of methylphenidate. The drug is released over the course of a day. Concerta was made to be difficult to abuse.

Contaminants   Substances left behind when drugs are made. They can be harmful and toxic (poisonous).

Controlled substance   A substance or medication that is restricted by law. Different degrees of control exist, based on how dangerous or abusable a drug is.

Crashing   The experience that occurs after many hours or days of drug use (bingeing), when an abuser becomes too tired to continue. Crashing often is associated with withdrawal symptoms.

Crystal meth   An illegal form of methamphetamine. *See* "Methamphetamine."

Crystal Meth Anonymous (CMA)   A treatment program based on the 12 steps of Narcotics Anonymous

(NA), but specific to crystal meth addiction. *See* "Narcotics Anonymous."

Daytrana A patch that contains methylphenidate. It is applied to the skin and used to treat ADHD.

Decongestant A drug that helps to unplug the nose. Decongestants are used to treat the symptoms of a cold. Pseudoephedrine is the most common example.

Delirium A condition that can cause restlessness, excitement, hallucinations, and delusions. Illness or drug use may lead to delirium.

Delusional parasitosis A type of delusion that is common in meth users. People with delusional parasitosis believe that they are covered in bugs.

Delusions Brain changes that cause people to believe things that are not true. *See* "Delusional Parasitosis."

Dendrites Short nerve fibers that receive messages from nearby neurons. After receiving a message, a dendrite sends it to the cell body.

Dependence The condition that occurs when a person's body becomes used to the effects of a drug. When that person tries to stop using the drug, his or her body does not function as well as it did while the person was using the drug.

Desoxyn The legal form of methamphetamine. It is manufactured by drug companies and prescribed by doctors to treat a few medical conditions, including narcolepsy.

Dexedrine Another name for dextroamphetamine. *See* "Dextroamphetamine."

Dexmethylphenidate A medicine related to methylphenidate. It is used to treat ADHD. *See* "Focalin."

Dextroamphetamine A type of amphetamine commonly known as Dextrostat or Dexedrine. It is used legally to treat certain medical conditions, including ADHD and narcolepsy.

Dextrostat Another name for dextroamphetamine. *See* "Dextroamphetamine."

Dopamine The most important neurotransmitter affected by stimulant drugs. Dopamine is released during rewarding activities and causes feelings of excitement and pleasure.

Doping Is used to describe the use of drugs or banned substances by athletes to enhance their physical performance or to gain a competitive edge.

Drug paraphernalia Items used to administer drugs. Such items include syringes and drug pipes.

Drug schedules Categories used to classify drugs based on how dangerous or how widely abused they are. The United States has five drug schedules. Canada has eight. These schedules are also used to determine punishments for possessing, selling, and making drugs.

Ecstasy An illegal drug that is addictive and widely abused. It is made in clandestine labs. It is often considered a "party drug" because of its use in the rave and dance scenes.

Ephedrine A stimulant drug that is found in some herbal products and energy drinks. It is sold legally in small amounts, but it can be deadly if it is abused. Ephedrine is used to treat asthma and colds. It is also used to produce crystal meth.

Euphoria An intense feeling of pleasure, happiness, and well-being. A desire for euphoria is the reason some people abuse stimulant drugs. Drug-caused euphoria does not last long, and people need to use more and more of a drug to get the same feeling of euphoria that they got the first time.

Exporting The act of transporting drugs out of a country for the purpose of illegal trafficking.

Fight-or-flight response An increased heart rate, expanded airways, increased muscle fuel, and dilated pupils. These changes are caused by increases in a neurotransmitter called norepinephrine. The changes allow the body to respond to a threat or other emergency by either staying to fight or running away (flight).

Focalin   A drug that contains dexmethylphenidate. Its effects are similar to those of methylphenidate. Focalin is used to treat ADHD.

Food and Drug Administration (FDA)   A division of the U.S. government's Department of Health and Human Services that regulates the release of new drugs and drug products.

Hallucinations   A symptom that may result from stimulant abuse. A person having hallucinations sees and hears things that are not real.

High   The feeling of being intoxicated that occurs when a drug is abused. Stimulant abusers often report being high as feeling very energetic and happy.

Ice   Another name for methamphetamine produced on the street. This term is usually used to describe the pure, clear, and crystal-like form of the drug.

Importing   The act of transporting drugs into a country for the purpose of selling them illegally.

Insomnia   A state of being tired, but not being able to fall asleep or stay asleep.

Manufacture   The process of making a drug. Drugs can be manufactured legally (by pharmaceutical companies) or illegally (by street chemists in clandestine labs).

MDMA (methylenedioxymethamphetamine)   Another name for Ecstasy. *See* "Ecstasy."

Meridia   A stimulant drug that is often used to treat obesity. Compared with other stimulants, Meridia is safer and less addictive.

Metabolize   To break down food or drugs into other substances within the body.

Metadate   A form of methylphenidate that contains immediate-acting and long-acting beads of the drug in a capsule. This form allows for quick but long-lasting relief of ADHD symptoms.

Meth   *See* "Methamphetamine."

Methamphetamine   An addictive and dangerous stimulant drug that is found in legal (Desoxyn) and illegal (crystal meth) forms. Methamphetamine is used legally to treat conditions such as narcolepsy. Abuse of the drug is well documented. It is known on the street by many names, including meth, crystal meth, and ice.

Meth lab   *See* "Clandestine lab."

Meth mouth   Severe tooth decay and gum disease caused by methamphetamine abuse. Users' teeth often break off or must be pulled.

Methylin   A type of methylphenidate. It is used to treat ADHD and is available as a liquid, a regular tablet, or a chewable tablet.

Methylphenidate   A stimulant drug commonly known as Ritalin. It is used legally to treat ADHD and other conditions, including narcolepsy. Other drugs that contain methylphenidate include Concerta, Focalin, Metadate and Methylin. Methylphenidate may be addictive and is associated with abuse.

Mom-and-pop lab   A smaller and fairly common type of lab in which illegal drugs are produced. A mom and pop lab can produce 1–2 ounces (30–60 g) of methamphetamine per day.

Narcolepsy   A condition that causes people to fall asleep quickly and at unusual times, such as while driving. The condition is treated with stimulant medicines.

Narcotics Anonymous (NA)   A 12-step program designed to help people stop using drugs. It centers on meetings that are attended by drug users and former drug users. These meetings provide abusers with a support system and guidelines to follow.

Neuron   A cell in the brain that receives and sends signals that control body functions.

Neurotransmitter reuptake   A recycling process that occurs when neurotransmitters are released into a synapse (space) between neurons. Reuptake happens when transmitters are taken up again by the neuron that released them.

Neurotransmitters   Chemical messengers in the brain that move information from one cell to another. Stimulant drugs affect three neurotransmitters: dopamine, serotonin, and norepinephrine.

Nicotine   A stimulant drug found in cigarettes and chewing tobacco, both of which are sold legally. Nicotine is very addictive.

Norepinephrine   A neurotransmitter that is released when stimulant drugs are used. Norepinephrine controls the fight-or-flight response, which determines how a person will act in stressful or threatening situations.

Nucleus   The part of a neuron that directs the traffic of the cell. The cell's nucleus makes sense of messages coming from the dendrites, and then passes the messages on to the axon.

Orally   By mouth.

Overdose   To take too much of a drug. An overdose can be deadly and needs to be treated immediately. Stimulant overdose may cause confusion, paranoia, psychosis, aggression, seizures, and strokes.

Paranoia   A type of delusion that causes people to believe falsely that others around them want to hurt them or get them into trouble. Paranoid people do not trust anyone.

Parent drug   A drug used to research and design other new drugs.

Patent   A document giving the inventor of a product the exclusive rights to use, make, and sell that product for a certain period of time.

Peripheral effects   Effects that involve the heart, muscles, and other non–nervous-system tissues of the body. Changes in peripheral effects can lead to a faster heart rate, shakiness, and increased muscle movements.

Possession   The legal term used to describe people who are found to have illegal drugs for their personal use.

Prescription forgeries   Fake prescriptions or prescriptions that have been changed. People forge prescriptions to get drugs from a pharmacy without stealing them.

Pseudoephedrine   A stimulant drug found in many cold and flu medicines. It helps to unplug the nose. It can be dangerous if it is not used properly. It is used as an ingredient in crystal meth.

Psychosis   A disturbance in the mind that causes people to lose touch with reality. People with psychosis can experience changes in the way that they see, hear, and understand the world around them. Psychosis is often associated with delusions and hallucinations.

Purify   To remove contaminants from a product.

Receptors   Special bonding sites on the dendrites of cells. Neurotransmitters bind to receptors to pass on messages.

Reinforcing effects   The pleasurable feelings caused by a drug. These feelings make a person want to take the drug again.

Ritalin   A stimulant drug used to treat ADHD. Ritalin was the first drug on the market to contain methylphenidate. It is still the best-known form of methylphenidate. It is now also available as Ritalin-SR (sustained release) and Ritalin-LA (long acting). *See* "Methylphenidate."

Schedules   *See* "Drug schedules."

Self-treat   To treat a real illness with a drug that has not been prescribed by a doctor. The drugs people choose for self-treatment may be legal or illegal. People often self-treat ADHD with stimulants, for example.

Serotonin   A neurotransmitter that is released in the brain when stimulant drugs are taken. The release of serotonin leads to good feelings. Serotonin also can cause changes in vision or in the way things feel.

Sexually transmitted diseases (STDs)   Diseases spread through unprotected sex. Hepatitis C, HIV (the AIDS virus), gonorrhea, and chlamydia are examples of STDs. The risk of spreading and getting an STD is higher in drug users. People who use drugs often are less careful about protection and may have sex with a number of different partners.

Sibutramine   *See* "Meridia."

Smuggle   To import or export items such as drugs illegally and secretly.

Speed bumps   Red bumps or rashes that develop on the skin of stimulant users. The bumps sometimes appear where drugs have been injected, but they can be found anywhere on the body.

Stimulant   Stimulant drugs include caffeine, nicotine, cocaine, Ecstasy, amphetamines, methamphetamine, and methylphenidate. These drugs work by increasing chemical signalers in the brain. They can be mild, like caffeine, or strong and dangerous. Stimulants cause a person to have more energy, an increased heart rate, and increased blood pressure. Some stimulants can cause paranoia, hallucinations, and even death.

Street chemist   A person who makes illegal drugs in clandestine labs.

Superlab   A large meth lab. Superlabs can produce more then 10 pounds (4.5 kg) of methamphetamine per day.

Synapse   The tiny gap between the axon of one neuron and the dendrites of another neuron.

Talwin   A prescription painkiller that is often abused by being mixed with Ritalin. The combination produces a high similar to the high from mixing heroin and cocaine.

Tolerance   The state of becoming used to a drug. As tolerance develops, a person must use more and more of the drug to get the same effects.

Track marks   Bruises and needle marks left on the body by repeated injections of drugs.

Transdermal patch system   A drug-filled patch that is applied to the skin. The drug passes from the patch to the skin and through the skin into the body.

Trafficking   Selling drugs to other people.

Tweaking   Behavior that occurs when people are high on stimulants. When someone is tweaking, he or she often feels the need to repeat certain actions over and over again. A common example of tweaking is taking apart and rebuilding electronic devices.

Withdrawal   Happens when a person stops taking a drug after becoming dependent on it. Withdrawal causes powerful feelings such as anger, depression, thoughts of suicide, and a strong desire to get more of the drug. Withdrawal often is more difficult if a user has been injecting or smoking a drug.

BIBLIOGRAPHY

BOOKS

Bayer, Linda., McCafferty, Barry., Jaffe, Steven. *Amphetamines & Other Uppers*. Philadelphia: Chelsea House Publishers, 2000.

Clayton, Lawrence. *Amphetamines & Other Stimulants*. New York: Rosen Publishing Group, 1998.

Diller, Lawrence. *Running on Ritalin: A Physician Reflects on Children, Society, and Performance in a Pill*. New York: Bantam Books, 1988.

Ferreiro, Carmen. *Ritalin and Other Methylphenidate-Containing Drugs*. New York: Infobase Publishing, 2004.

Koda-Kimble, Mary Anne and Young Lloyd Yee. *Applied Therapeutics: The Clinical Use of Drugs*, 8th ed. Philadelphia: Lippincott Williams & Wilkins, 2004.

ARTICLES

AJ, George. "Central Nervous System Stimulants." *Bailliere's Best Practice & Research. Clinical Endocrinology & Metabolism* 14(1) (2000): 79–88.

Ambrose, Peter. "Drug Use in Sports: A Veritable Arena for Pharmacists." *Journal of the American Pharmacists Association* 44(4) (2004): 501–516.

Barr, Alasdair M., Panenka, William J., et al. "The Need for Speed: An Update on Methamphetamine Addiction." *Journal of Psychiatry and Neuroscience* 31 (2006): 301–313.

Barrett, Sean P., Darredeau, Christine., et al. "Characteristics of Methylphenidate Misuse in a University Student Sample." *Canadian Journal of Psychiatry* 50 (2005): 457–461.

Cretzmeyer, Margaret, Vaughan Sarrazin Mary et al. "Treatment of Methamphetamine Abuse: Research Findings and Clinical Directions." *Journal of Substance Abuse Treatment* 24 (2003): 267–277.

Doyle, D. "Adolf Hitler's Medical Care." *Journal of the Royal College of Physicians of Edinburgh* 35 (2005): 75–82.

Hanson, Glen R., Rau, Kristi S., et al. "The Methamphet-amine Experience: A NIDA Partnership." *Neuropharmacology* 47 (2004): 92–100.

Karch, Steven B. "Cocaine: History, Use, Abuse." *Journal of the Royal Society of Medicine* 92 (1999): 393–397.

Milroy C.M. "Ten Years of 'Ecstasy'." *Journal of the Royal Society of Medicine* 92 (1999): 68–72.

Romanelli, Frank and Kelly M. Smith. "Clinical Effects and Management of Methamphetamine Abuse." *Pharmacotherapy* 26 (2006): 1148–1156.

Sajan, Amin.., Corneil, Trevor, et al. "The Street Value of Prescription Drugs." *Canadian Medical Association Journal* 159 (1998):139–142.

Sappell, Joel and Robert W. Welkos. "Suits, Protests Fuel a Campaign Against Psychiatry." *The Los Angeles Times* 29 June 1990: A48:1.

Volkow, Nora D. and James M. Swanson. "Variables That Affect the Clinical Use and Abuse of Methylphenidate in the Treatment of ADHD." *American Journal of Psychiatry* 160 (2003): 1909–1918.

WEB SITES

"2006 World Drug Report. Volume 2: Statistics." United Nations Office on Drugs and Crime. 2006. URL: http://www.unodc.org/pdf/WDR_2006/wdr2006_volume2.pdf.

Canadian Centre on Substance Abuse. URL: http://www.ccsa.ca/ccsa.

"Children in Methamphetamine 'Labs' in Oregon." CD Summary: An Epidemiology Publication of the Oregon Department of Human Services. August 12, 2003. URL: http://egov.oregon.gov/DHS/ph/cdsummary/2003/ohd5216.pdf.

"Child's death strikes at heart of small Indiana town." WHAS11.com. February 6, 2005. URL: http://www.whas11.com/topstories/stories/020505ccjrwhascollmanreax.7c527515.html.

"Controlled Drugs and Substances Act." Department of Justice Canada. March 26, 2007. URL: http://laws.justice. gc.ca/en/C-38.8/index.html.

"Controlled Substances Act." U.S. Drug Enforcement Administration. September 13, 2006. URL: http://www.dea.gov/ pubs/csa.html.

"Court Reverses Mom's Meth Baby Murder Conviction." USA Today. September 22, 2005. URL: http://www.usatoday. com/news/nation/2005-09-22-methmurderconviction_ x.htm.

CrystalMeth BC. Project of the Crystal Meth Victoria Society. URL: http://www.crystalmethbc.com/.

"DEA: Drug Traffickers used Elmo Dolls to Conceal Meth." U.S. Drug Enforcement Administration. October 25, 2006. URL: http://www.dea.gov/pubs/states/newsrel/denver102506.html.

"A Dictionary of Slang Drug Terms, Trade Names, and Pharmacological Effects and Uses." Texas Commission on Alcohol and Drug Abuse. October 1997. URL: http://www. tcada.state.tx.us/research/slang/terms.pdf.

"Do You Know…Amphetamines." Centre for Addiction and Mental Health. 2004. URL: http://www.camh.net/About_ Addiction_Mental_Health/Drug_and_Addiction_ Information/amphetamines_dyk.html.

"The Drug Situation Report, 2005." Royal Canadian Mounted Police. December 2006. URL: http://www.rcmp-grc.gc.ca/crimint/drugs_2005_e.htm.

Drug Use Among Ontario Students – 1977-2005. Centre for Addiction and Mental Health. October 2005. URL: http://www.camh.net/Research/Areas_of_research/Population_Life_Course_Studies/OSDUS/OSDUS2005_Highlights-Drug_final.pdf.

"Drug Use in Sport". Australian Sports Drug Agency. 2001. URL: http://www.smartplay.net/moves/drugs/drugsinfo. html.

DrugInfo Clearinghouse. Australian Drug Foundation. URL: http://www.druginfo.adf.org.au.

"Economic and Social Consequences of Drug Abuse and Illicit Trafficking." United Nations Office on Drugs and Crime. 1998. URL: http://www.unodc.org/pdf/technical_series_1998-01-01_1.pdf.

"Ephedrine Under Baseball's Microscope." USA Today. February 20, 2003. URL: http://www.usatoday.com/sports/baseball/2003-02-20-cover-ephedrine-baseball_x.htm.

"Facts & Figures: Methamphetamine." U.S. Office of National Drug Control Policy. March 21, 2007. URL: http://www.whitehousedrugpolicy.gov/drugfact/methamphetamine/index.html.

Medline Plus. U.S. National Library of Medicine and the National Institutes of Health. Drug Information for Amphetamines, Dexmethylphenidate, Methylphenidate, and Methylphenidate Transdermal. Accessed Feb 5, 2007. Available at: http://medlineplus.gov.

"Meth and Crime." Illinois Attorney General. March 2007. URL: http://www.illinoisattorneygeneral.gov/methnet/understandingmeth/crime.html.

"The Meth Diet—Not FDA Approved!" University of Iowa Student Health Service. May 12, 2004. URL: http://www.uistudenthealth.com/question/default.asp?asgid=5&agid=1&id=477.

Meth—Not Even Once. Montana Meth Project. URL: http://www.notevenonce.com.

"Methamphetamine." U.S. Drug Enforcement Administration. June 2006. URL: http://www.deadiversion.usdoj.gov/drugs_concern/meth.htm.

"Heavy Metal and Organic Contaminants Associated with Illicit Methamphetamine Production." *Methamphetamine Abuse: Epidemiologic Issues and Implications*. National Institute on Drug Abuse Research Monograph 115, p. 47+. 1991. URL: http://www.drugabuse.gov/pdf/monographs/download115.html.

"Methamphetamine Abuse and Addiction." National Institute on Drug Abuse Research Report Series. NIH Publication Number 06-4210. Last revised September 2006. URL: http://www.nida.nih.gov/PDF/RRMetham.pdf.

"Methamphetamine Drug Threat Assessment." U.S. National Drug Intelligence Center. March 2005. URL: http://www.usdoj.gov/ndic/pubs11/13853/index.htm.

"My Life with Meth: Forty Tennesseans Share Their Stories." Tennessee District Attorney's General Conference. May 3, 2006. URL: http://www.methfreetn.org/pdf/MethStories-Booklet.pdf.

"National Drug Threat Assessment 2007: Methamphetamine." National Drug Intelligence Center. October 2006. URL: http://www.usdoj.gov/ndic/pubs21/21137/meth.htm.

"National Drug Threat Assessment 2007: Pharmaceutical Drugs." National Drug Intelligence Center. October 2006. URL: http://www.usdoj.gov/ndic/pubs21/21137/pharm.htm.

"Neuroscience of psychoactive substance use and dependence." World Health Organization. 2004. URL: http://www.who.int/substance_abuse/publications/en/Neuroscience.pdf.

"NIDA for Teens: Mind Over Matter." National Institute on Drug Abuse. January 12, 2007. URL: http://www.teens.drugabuse.gov/mom/index.asp.

"NIDA InfoFacts: Methylphenidate (Ritalin)." National Institute on Drug Abuse. May 2006. URL: http://www.nida.nih.gov/pdf/infofacts/Ritalin06.pdf.

"NIDA InfoFacts: Nationwide Trends." National Institute on Drug Abuse. September 2004. URL: http://www.nida.nih.gov/pdf/infofacts/NationTrends.pdf.

"Organized Crime in Canada: A Quarterly Summary." Nathanson Centre on Transnational Human Rights, Crime, and Security. April–June 2005. URL: http://www.yorku.ca/nathanson/CurrentEvents/2005_Q2.htm.

"Prescription Drug Abuse Chart." National Institute on Drug Abuse. February 2007. URL: http://www.nida.nih.gov/Drug-Pages/PrescripDrugsChart.html.

"Preventing Drug Use Among Children and Adolescents: A Research-based Guide for Parents, Educators and Community Leaders." National Institute on Drug Abuse. Second Edition. October 2003. URL: http://www.drugabuse.gov/pdf/prevention/RedBook.pdf.

"State of the Knowledge: Methamphetamine." HereToHelp: British Columbia Partners for Mental Health and Addictions Information. 2004. URL: http://www.heretohelp.bc.ca/publications/stateofknowledge/methamphetamine.pdf.

"Street Terms: Drugs and the Drug Trade: Ritalin." Office of National Drug Control Policy. August 2006. URL: http://www.whitehousedrugpolicy.gov/streetterms/ByType.asp?intTypeID=55.

"Substance Abuse Treatment Facility Locator." Substance Abuse & Mental Health Services Administration. March 2007. URL: http://dasis3.samhsa.gov/

"Teen Herbicide." Mother Jones. May/June 2003. URL: http://www.motherjones.com/news/outfront/2003/05/ma_378_01.html?welcome=true.

"Vikings: Stringer's use of ephedra contributed to death." Sports Illustrated.com. February 25, 2003. URL: http://sportsillustrated.cnn.com/football/news/2003/02/25/stringer_ephedra_ap/.

"Young People in Canada: Their Health and Well-Being. Chapter 6: Youth Health Risk Behaviors." Public Health Agency of Canada, Division of Childhood and Adolescence. October 2004. URL: http://www.phac-aspc.gc.ca/dca-dea/publications/hbsc-2004/chapter_6_e.html.

FURTHER READING

Ferreiro, Carmen, et al. *Ritalin and Other Methylphenidate-Containing Drugs*. New York: Chelsea House, 2004.

Fitzhugh, Karla. *Crystal Meth and Other Amphetamines (What's the Deal?)*. Chicago: Heinemann, 2005.

Harris, Nancy. *The History of Drugs – Amphetamines*. San Diego: Greenhaven Press, 2004.

Marcovitz, Hal. *Methamphetamine*. San Diego: Lucent Books, 2005.

Spalding, Frank. *Methamphetamine: The Dangers of Crystal Meth (Drug Abuse & Society: Cost to a Nation)*. New York: Rosen Publishing Group, 2006.

Roffe Menhard, Francha. *The Facts About Amphetamines*. New York: Benchmark Books, 2006.

Roffe Menhard, Francha. *The Facts About Ritalin*. New York: Benchmark Books, 2006.

WEB SITES

NIDA FOR TEENS: THE SCIENCE BEHIND DRUG ABUSE

On this Web site, teens can learn about many drugs, including nicotine and other stimulants. They can also read about other teens' real-life experiences with drugs and can participate in interactive learning games and quizzes.

http://teens.drugabuse.gov/

JUST THINK TWICE

This Web site, which is run by the U.S. Drug Enforcement Agency (DEA), provides teens with information about drugs of abuse. It is visually appealing and interactive. The site gives accurate and current information about the costs to society of drug use, drug use rates, and the dangers of drug abuse.

http://www.justthinktwice.com/

MONTANA METH PROJECT

This Web site discusses the dangers of methamphetamine abuse and how to seek help. It also includes stories from users and their friends and families. Teens can watch video clips and listen to ads that have been broadcast on TV and radio.

http://www.notevenonce.com/

US DEPARTMENT OF HEALTH AND HUMAN SERVICES AND SAMHSA'S NATIONAL CLEARINGHOUSE FOR ALCOHOL AND DRUG INFORMATION: TIPS FOR TEENS

This Web site provides facts for teens about methamphetamine. It discusses warning signs and how meth affects your body. It also provides links to other useful information, including a drug usage expense calculator.

http://ncadi.samhsa.gov/govpubs/PHD861/

KCI: THE ANTI-METH SITE

This Web site provides basic information about methamphetamine and has links to other useful sites and information. The site has a large archive of stories that have been submitted by users and their loved ones. It also has a message board and a chat room.

www.kci.org

PICTURE CREDITS

INDEX

ABOUT THE AUTHORS

LIANNE WARBURTON and **DIANA CALLFAS** graduated with Bachelor of Science degrees in Pharmacy from the University of Saskatchewan in Canada. They currently are community pharmacists in Canada. Over the past few years, they have researched, developed, and piloted a crystal methamphetamine educational program geared toward adolescents and their parents. The program is intended to dispel myths, increase awareness, and educate people about the dangers associated with the use of this destructive drug. Warburton and Callfas also have been keynote speakers at a number of conferences related to the topic of crystal meth abuse. The majority of these conferences have focused on educating health-care professionals. Warburton and Callfas have provided a pharmacist's perspective to many different audiences and have participated in many workshops. In May of 2005, the Saskatchewan College of Pharmacists awarded Warburton and Callfas the college's Presidential Citation for their work.

Series introduction author **RONALD J. BROGAN** is the Bureau Chief for the New York City office of D.A.R.E. (Drug Abuse Resistance Education) America, where he trains and coordinates more than 100 New York City police officers in program-related activities. He also serves as a D.A.R.E. regional director for Oregon, Connecticut, Massachusetts, Maine, New Hampshire, New York, Rhode Island, and Vermont. In 1997, Brogan retired from the U.S. Drug Enforcement Administration (DEA), where he served as a special agent for 26 years. He holds bachelor's and master's degrees in criminal justice from the City University of New York.